Clergyman's
Psychological Handbook

Reprinted, July 1978

Copyright © 1974 by Wm. B. Eerdmans Publishing Co.
All rights reserved
Printed in the United States of America

Library of Congress Cataloging in Publication Data

McLemore, Clinton W   1946-
  Clergyman's psychological handbook.

  Bibliography: pp. 44f., 70f., 97f., 136f.
  1. Pastoral counseling.   I.   Title.
BV4012.2.M24   253.5   74-2011
ISBN 0-8028-1576-6

To Alicia, Gregory, and Karl —
who make it all worthwhile

Acknowledgments

I can hardly contain my joy at this opportunity to thank publicly the people who in one way or another significantly contributed to this book. It grew out of my several years of collaboration and friendship with the Reverend Dan L. Ballinger, who has continually shown me God's character and taught me the meaning of the word "ministry." Professionally, I owe my greatest debt to my friend, colleague, and teacher, Dr. Philip Alden Smith. In writing this book I have become aware of how my ideas and even my phrases frequently reflect the countless hours he and I have worked together. He has constructively commented on parts of the manuscript, as has my close friend, Bryant B. Crouse, whom I take pleasure in pointing out as a thoroughly gifted, rising young colleague in my profession.

Several other people have been particularly helpful. Sister Mary Frederick Arnold, C. S. J., chairman of the Psychology Department at Mount St. Mary's College, has been fully supportive and has made my years at the college most enjoyable. Sister Mary Patricia Sexton, C. S. J., has given valuable technical advice on parts of the writing. And Mrs. Joan Mital provided competent secretarial services and typed the final manuscript.

Finally, I acknowledge and honor my late father, Eugene McLemore, for teaching me that a man can usually do what he thinks he can, and my mother, Clara G. McLemore, for loving me without ceasing.

C. W. M.

Preface

This handbook meets the need for practical answers to many of the front-line problems pastoral counselors see every day. In one handy volume, Dr. McLemore systematizes the wide range of clinical problems clergymen encounter and presents hundreds of tips on how to meet such challenges. He has also included analyses of theoretical concepts of counseling, guidelines on how to use professional consultants, and discussion of how to assess the clinical and pastoral services needed by particular individuals. The possession and use of this handbook is like having a close, consulting relationship with a clinical psychologist who is interested in and familiar with the kinds of counseling dilemmas those of us in the ministry face.

Those who read this book will find themselves acquainted with a professionally trained scholar and clinician who is deeply committed to the view of human life that was given to us by Jesus. Part of this view is that every human being is of incalculable worth; that the encouragement of the human soul is the noblest work among men; that relationships are sacred and worth great cost to preserve; that God's Kingdom is uniquely composed of those people who own their feelings, their sin, and their responsibility to choose the kinds of persons they will be; and that wisdom applied to this choosing is one of the great, aching needs of our century. This counseling text is a particularly useful encouragement to those of us whose work it is to encourage.

I commend this book to you, confident that in its using, you will find a friend at your side who is thorough and prepared in his dedication to helping you become a better pastor to those in your charge.

Dan Ballinger, Minister
Community Christian Church
Inglewood, California

Contents

IV. SPECIAL TECHNIQUES AND PROBLEMS 99

Introduction

As a ministering clergyman, you are subject to demands and expectations that would oppress most psychologists and psychiatrists. You encounter the whole spectrum of psychological disorders and do not enjoy the liberty of "screening your practice." You are always "on call" but most likely do not have the protection of either an answering service, conveniently scheduled appointments, or surcharges for emergency consultations at inopportune times. And almost invariably you are counted on by someone — friend, relative, or the individual himself — to bring about a "cure." Furthermore, like most clergymen, you are probably regarded much like a parent, with a variable mixture of affection, dependency, mistrust, and fear. Often the counselee's ambivalence makes difficult the development of a helping relationship, thus imposing formidable burdens on your skill and endurance. Finally, a clergyman is supposed to be charitable, by which people usually mean that you should give physically and emotionally without limit and with no view toward tangible reward.

I have written this handbook to provide you with the practical knowledge necessary to meet these demands. To this end I have included discussions of: the various psychological disorders; general evaluation procedures; interviewing and counseling techniques; special therapeutic treatments such as psychiatric medication and behavior therapy; the use of consultants like psychologists, psychiatric physicians, and social workers; management of difficult problems such as alcoholism and suicide threats; methods of group counseling; and a number of procedural tips such as when to involve the person's family, record keeping, when and to whom to refer clients, and how often to schedule counseling sessions. Annotated recommended readings appear at the end of each chapter. I have listed a few good resource books rather than amassing a large bibliography through which you would have to sift. Less than twenty years ago this book would have been considered too technical for most clergymen. Its emphasis on psychological disorder and remediation might have seemed inappropriate, and the suggestion that clergymen do many of the same things as psychotherapists might have miffed the secular professional community. But with fewer than 40,000 credentialed therapists in the nation, mental health professionals are increasingly aware of the important contributions made by local clergymen, whom they have come to recognize as valuable allies. In fact, it is becoming clearer all the time that clergymen, together with family physicians, carry the bulk of the nation's psychological services burden.

Today's clergyman is no longer without formal psychological training. Seminaries and other religious educational institutions are offering a wide range of psychosocial studies, including courses in abnormal psychology and advanced counseling. Pastoral clergymen are finding good use for many of the ideas and procedures that secular professionals have developed, and they are no longer satisfied with cliches as guidelines on how to do their counseling.

I have tried to make this book as conversational as possible. If you had asked me to sit by the fire and tell you what I believed would prove helpful to you in your pastoral counseling, I would have said the things I've written here.

CHAPTER I

MODES OF DYSFUNCTION

Organic and Functional Disorders
Diagnosis
Normality
Mental Illness
Development of Disordered Behavior
Functional Disorders
Organic Disorders

WHEN A PERSON comes to you as his clergyman, he usually wants some kind of assistance. And often the help he requests is in some sense psychological. He wants to know what you think of sending his child to a private school, or if you know a good doctor to treat an aging aunt. Should a woman call the police the next time her husband beats her? Should a retired missionary pray three minutes after meals or is two minutes sufficient? Do we need marriage counseling, or can we work things out on our own? What can I do about my nervousness? About my need for alcohol? About my frigidity? What about my daughter who keeps irritating me, or my youngest son who's failing in school? Most clergymen could expand this list indefinitely. But how does one respond to these problems?

In the past, psychiatrists and psychologists tightly guarded what they considered to be their professional domains and failed to realize that a clergyman does a great deal of front-line clinical service. Today, however, clinicians recognize the clergyman as a professional colleague who can use and, in fact, needs to know a considerable amount of serious psychology. Accordingly, throughout this book I will present specific evaluation and counseling procedures. In this chapter, I would like to sketch the boundaries of what we will be dealing with by presenting a compendium of how practicing clinicians organize and classify the different psychological disorders. Such a conceptual framework, a way of viewing human problems, will assist you in thinking about psychological dysfunction and will help you decide how best to aid particular individuals with their difficulties.

Organic and Functional Disorders

Clinicians divide psychological disorders into two main categories, those which can be attributed directly to physical abnormalities and those which cannot. Problems for which no biological cause can be specified are termed "functional," indicating that they do not appear to be due to organic pathology. Although it is necessary to be alert for signs of neurological impairment or other physical ailments, so that prompt referral to a physician can be arranged (see Chapter Three), most persons you will see for counseling have problems in living rather than diseases of the endocrine glands or the central nervous system. Biological predispositions may contribute to the development of functional difficulties but their effects are unspecifiable and probably secondary. Opinion differs on the importance of physiology to psychological dysfunction, especially when it comes to the more serious disorders, but the organic-functional distinction is useful in highlighting the difference between physically and psychologically based disorders, an issue to which I shall return shortly.

Diagnosis

Systematic classifications of disorders can help you decide whether to work with a particular person or to refer him, what the outcome of your work is likely to be, and what approaches and techniques might be of most benefit. But bear in mind that diagnostic systems in psychology and psychiatry are largely a matter of convenience and tradition. For example, the term schizophrenia (which incidentally does not mean two personalities but a pronounced split between thought and feeling) has been applied to a wide variety of behaviors. Unlike many medical disorders, there are no clear-cut laboratory tests to confirm or disconfirm such a diagnosis. No one really knows whether schizophrenia is best conceived of as one problem manifesting itself in various ways or as several different and essentially unrelated problems. Psychologists speak of from four to twelve types of schizophrenia, but they may be lumping together fundamentally different syndromes. Twenty years from now, clinicians may be using a different classification system. So try to keep in mind that psychiatric labels do not immutably characterize persons to whom they are applied.

It has been customary in psychiatry and psychology to try to fit the "patient" into the "correct" diagnostic category. This is an unfortunate carry-over from medicine, where an individual is likely to have only one of several possible diseases. Such a practice is inappropriate in psychology, since psychiatric diagnoses do not necessarily signify distinct underlying diseases and, for the most part, are merely descriptive labels. A particular person might fit into several categories equally well, so that a quest for *the* right diagnosis is misguided.

Normality

There is no universally accepted definition of psychological normality. Experts are far from agreeing on the characteristics of an optimally functioning person, and consensus is more easily reached on the nature of abnormality. Consequently, psychological well-being is usually defined as the absence of problems. However, for practical purposes you can regard a person as normal who:

maintains mutually satisfying interpersonal relationships

does not frequently speak or act peculiarly or bizarrely

shows awareness of and accepts responsibility for his* own actions and feelings, including negative emotions like anger

realistically appraises the assets and limitations of himself and others and does not make unreasonable demands on either

shows both emotional spontaneity and control

does not display recurrent self-defeating behavior patterns

expresses his emotional needs honestly rather than at-

---

*Or her. In the absence of genderless substitutes, he, his, and him are used in this book as singular pronouns. It is to be understood that both women and men are addressed as counselors and assumed as counselees.

tempting to manipulate others into fulfilling them.

Probably no one meets all these criteria all the time —
normality is a matter of one's batting average.

Mental Illness

Historically, the conceptualization of emotional problems
as diseases served an important social function. Disturbed
persons had long been objects of ridicule and brutality.
Since people were accustomed to treating the sick with
kindness and concern, getting the public to view troubled
persons as ill significantly lightened the burden of persecution such persons suffered. But this notion has outlived
much of its usefulness and now, instead of facilitating ad-
vances in remediation procedures, it maintains outmoded
ideas and practices. Most psychological disorders are best
regarded as products of unfavorable experiences and faulty
learning rather than as products of physical disease. The
term "illness" should be reserved for individuals whose
problems can be traced to a specific biological defect or
ailment, such as a brain lesion, barbiturate poisoning, or
neurosyphilis. Some of the more serious functional disorders, such as schizophrenia, may involve an underlying
genetic predisposition; but regardless of such a predis-
posing factor, it is unlikely that anyone would actually
develop the disorder without experiencing substantial environmental stress.

Development of Disordered Behavior

Before cataloging the various psychological disorders, I
would like to discuss some of the ways that people develop
personal problems. It is easy to be baffled by someone's
disturbance because often it is complex and one is hard
pressed to see how it originated. Sometimes the problem
seems to have come out of nowhere, and most of us tend
to look for a single cause. For example, the parents of one
boy kept asking if his problems were not due to a brain
tumor. Possibly this boy had such a tumor, but medical
examination showed no evidence for anything of the sort.

Furthermore, a tumor might have made him more volatile but could hardly have accounted for his complicated patterns of delinquent behavior. Sometimes people look not for an organic cause, but for a single traumatic event. The result is the same, an unduly simple explanation. Psychological disorders are learned, though faulty, motivations and behaviors which come about as the result of several converging processes. In this section I will summarize some of these processes.

Faulty Parental Models

Much of what someone becomes develops through imitation, by picking up the attributes of those around him. If we could always choose which behaviors to adopt and which to reject, many of us would be less troubled. Unfortunately, the imitation process is largely beyond our control. For example, a woman who despises her mother's cold vindictiveness and who herself tries to be warm and kind may still show her mother's negative qualities without realizing it. This "maternal introject" will be a source of baffling difficulties to her until she has the reconstructive experiences through which to free herself of her mother's internalized influence.

Consequence Training

People tend to do what they have found rewarding and to avoid doing what they have found unrewarding. Rewards and punishments effectively "stamp in" behavior. One might expect that behaviors which are no longer efficient or which lead to unpleasant consequences would drop out and that more adaptive behaviors would replace them. But this is not always the case. Presumably because of the many years over which certain behaviors have been reinforced, along with the erratic schedule under which this has occurred, many behavioral tendencies develop into enduring attributes of the personality. A child who learns to throw tantrums to prevent his parents from asking anxiety-provoking questions may find similar tactics as an adult to be costly. He might lose his job time after time without changing this behavior, partly because it has been so deeply ingrained and partly because he has not learned alternative behaviors.

Explicit and Implicit Instruction

A particular kind of consequence training involves, not the inadvertently learned behaviors mentioned above, but explicit instructions to act in specific ways, usually under threat of disapproval. Children are often trained to behave in ways that later prove dysfunctional. As an example, the child who is told to speak only when spoken to may have a lot of trouble asserting himself as an adult. Other kinds of instructions are less obvious. Parents frequently communicate expectations to their children without realizing it. For example, a parent who feels confined and inhibited by marriage may unwittingly encourage his child to act out his own fantasies of a more exciting life, which in turn might lead to delinquency which both parents would condemn. Another form of implicit instruction is manipulating conditions so as to leave the child with only one feasible alternative.

Autonomic Conditioning

Coming to associate one event with another so that a previously neutral event acquires the power to elicit physiological responses (classical conditioning) has received much attention from psychologists. Pets quickly learn to become attentive, to lick their lips, and to salivate when they hear the serving of their food. These responses, which normally occur during eating, become linked with stimulus events (e.g., the sound of the food being served) which would not ordinarily have elicited them. In a similar fashion, the perception of a parent would not, of itself, evoke fear. Yet, if the parent is routinely punitive, he or she may become a "conditional stimulus" for fear, which is a normal response to punishment. That is, the mere sight or sound of the parent may evoke fear in the child. Such conditioned fear may then generalize to all members of the parent's sex, establishing fundamental avoidance tendencies toward males or females. Of course, such conditioned emotional reactions and response tendencies can also be positive, involving approach rather than avoidance behavior.

Self-Instruction and Self-Reinforcement

I have already referred to parental introjects, collections of behaviors and beliefs incorporated more or less unconsciously into the personality. Therapists from Sigmund Freud to Albert Ellis and Fritz Perls have made much of how what parents communicate to a child, by way of expectations and evaluations, becomes internalized so that the child learns to say similar things to himself. Parents establish and convey attitudes toward the child as he is and as they would like him to be. They may regard him as fully acceptable only if he achieves outstandingly in sports or academics. Or they may accept him only if he is a conforming person who will do whatever his parents ask of him without question. In the course of growing up, the child comes to impose the same conditions for acceptance on himself, making self-esteem contingent on rigidly high levels of performance. It is worth noting that people carry on internal conversations of which they may be completely unaware, and that they have learned to tell themselves all sorts of unreasonable things.

These descriptions do not exhaust the processes by which behavior is acquired, but they do cover those which are most important. Imitation of models, consequence or reinforcement training (sometimes called operant conditioning), association learning (called classical conditioning), self-instruction, punishment, and subtle social-psychological transactions are the main ways behavior is acquired.

Functional Disorders

Traditional psychiatric diagnosis emphasizes present symptoms over underlying personality characteristics or interpersonal behavior. Basic categories include: neuroses, psychoses, personality disorders, psychophysiological disorders, and transient stress reactions.

Neurotic Disorders

Neurotic problems usually distress the individual, causing considerable anxiety which may be consciously experienced or expressed indirectly. In some way the person's life is impaired and he is aware that a psychological problem exists, thus showing contact with reality (adequate reality testing). No evidence of serious mental disorganization is present.

Of more importance perhaps than neurotic symptoms are neurotic lifestyles. These are difficult to recognize because they do not involve obvious problems such as pervasive anxiety, irrational fears, inappropriate concerns, disruptive moods, or troublesome preoccupations and behaviors. Rather, they consist of habitually self-defeating styles of relating to others and to oneself, which insidiously impair or prevent smooth living or interpersonal relationships. In short, they prevent enduring emotional intimacy or personal happiness. I will discuss these at length after first surveying the neurotic symptoms.

Neurotic anxiety: Intense anxiety or panic, not restricted to specific objects or circumstances (free-floating anxiety), which may occur in any situation or at any time.

Hysterical conversion: Involuntary, psychologically based (psychogenic) physical impairment for which there is no organic cause, including such symptoms as blindness, deafness, or paralysis; to be distinguished from psychophysiological (psychosomatic) disorders in which there are genuine physical ailments caused by emotional stress. Note the difference between the clinical and popular use of the term "hysterical."

Hysterical dissociation: Includes such difficulties as amnesia, sleepwalking (somnambulism), and the unusual syndrome of carrying on activities without awareness or even establishing a life in another city for a time, disconnected from one's prior existence (fugue states).

Phobias: Pronounced fear of an object or situation, which the person acknowledges as unreasonable; for example, fear of open spaces or fear of rabbits.

Obsessions and compulsions: One or both of the following: intrusive, troublesome thoughts which the person is unable to put out of his mind, or the need to perform the same peculiar action over and over. An example of an obsession would be recurring ideas of falling which disturb the individual but which he cannot evict from consciousness. A compulsion would be an intense need to straighten one's office many times a day, even when pressing tasks require prompt completion. If compulsions are not carried out, distressing anxiety ensues.

Neurotic depression: Excessive depression in reaction to the loss of a cherished possession or loved one, or as a manifestation of internal conflicts. Depression frequently accompanies "not knowing what to do" (freezing) or submerged anger which the person is afraid to express or admit to himself.

Neurasthenia and hypochondriasis: Neurasthenia is excessive, chronic and inappropriate fatigue, usually accompanied by underlying depression. Hypochondriasis is inordinate concern with one's health and/or continual fear that one has contracted a disease, despite medical reassurance.

Neurotic Lifestyles (Personality Neuroses)

Anyone who works as a counselor or therapist has had some experience with most of the disorders listed above. But these problems are not nearly as common as the neurotic life styles I will now discuss. Neurotic life styles have been variously termed character disorders, personality trait and pattern disturbances, or character and personality neuroses. They are usually longstanding styles, not easily altered. A circumscribed neurotic ailment is much less an enduring aspect of the person than is a personality neurosis. Since you will probably find yourself referring to this section in the course of your work, I have included comments on counseling persons with these difficulties.

Seclusive personality: Such persons are shy, withdrawn, oversensitive, and interpersonally distant. They are primarily motivated to avoid hurt rather than to obtain satisfaction, and often develop an exaggerated fondness for animals, nature, reading, or hobbies, all of which provide sanctuary from interpersonal threat and secondarily serve as substitutes for relationships with people. Seclusive persons typically appear bland and emotionally flat, and they find it difficult to socialize or to express feelings. Despite this appearance, they are usually active imaginers, and because of their reticence to communicate openly with others, their thinking frequently becomes idiosyncratic. Seclusive persons usually show up in counseling for some problem other than their avoidance or distant interpersonal style. Depression or family crisis are common reasons. Such persons are attuned to the counselor's every move and are quick to terminate counseling at the slightest indication of irritation or rejection. Work must proceed slowly lest they be scared off — the counselor must be prepared to accept gradual progress since communicating an expectation of or demand for rapid change will significantly alarm seclusive individuals. Because they are acutely vulnerable, efforts to draw them out quickly are likely to induce the feeling that they've said too much, precipitating panic and withdrawal. Gentle support is desirable but confrontation is not. Successful work with seclusive persons requires much skill, patience, and sensitivity.

Histrionic personality: These persons, usually women, are emotionally immature, manipulative, dramatic, and demanding. They actively attempt to maneuver others into fulfilling their needs rather than expressing these needs directly. Histrionic persons are frequently provocative sexually but seem unaware of their seductiveness and feel greatly misunderstood when it is pointed out. Sexuality and emotion, in or out of marriage, is used as a weapon rather than as a vehicle for love and enjoyment. Frigidity is not uncommon. Histrionic persons have difficulty acknowledging, within themselves or others, primitive emotions like anger, and are given to Pollyanna attitudes which protect them from having to face such feelings. However, these persons are quite capable of indirect hostility if not outright viciousness, so long as they do not have to assume or admit responsibility for it. Clinicians emphasize the inordinate use histrionic persons make of repression (unconsciously putting out of and keeping from awareness one's unacceptable thoughts, feelings, impulses, and motives) and denial (automatically refusing to acknowledge consciously the thoughts, feelings, impulses, and motives of others). Despite their occasional flair and sociability, these persons are fundamentally dependent. What sets them apart from other dependent persons is their highly manipulative style of obtaining support and their inability to confront feelings.

Histrionic personalities are usually good counseling investments since they are able to respond emotionally, at least on the surface, and can form an attachment to the counselor. But the counselor has some difficulties to manage since such a person will almost invariably try to (1) encourage the counselor sexually and then renounce him for any interest he may show, (2) direct the interview focus away from genuine feelings onto some complicated practical problem, (3) manipulate the counselor into giving unending praise or reassurance, or (4) embroil him in a tacky interpersonal mess with other people. In short, anything to stay away from deep, personal feelings. The counselor should gently but firmly hold his ground and stick to the serious business at hand, namely that of helping the person become comfortable with genuine feelings and of learning more direct ways to obtain satisfaction. Competently conducted group experiences (whether labeled encounter, growth, sensitivity, training, or therapy groups) are often helpful.

Obstructive personality: The primary psychological characteristic of the obstructive person is intense anger coupled with strong fears of directly expressing hostility. Because of these fears, he resorts to indirect expressions of anger, such as slamming doors, accidentally dropping valuable objects, pouting, foot-dragging, and other forms of passive aggression. When questioned about these behaviors, he stubbornly denies any hostile intent, which protects him from retaliation since ostensibly he did the best he could and certainly was not angry! Obstructive persons show a more or less fundamental fear of losing control. They regard themselves as potentially dangerous and use passivity as insurance against allowing this aspect of themselves to be engaged. People with other maladaptive personality styles also show passive-aggressive behavior, but with the obstructive personality, indirectly expressed hostility has become almost a trademark. After prolonged contact with such persons, friends, relatives, and employers tire of their obstructionism and often cut them off.

Counseling the obstructive person is simple in theory but not in practice. The main objectives are to: (1) reduce his fear of directly expressing anger; (2) perhaps reduce the intensity of this anger; and (3) work with his fear of losing control. The first objective can be facilitated by assertive training (see the Behavior Therapy section of Chapter Four) in which the counselee practices directly expressing his irritation. For these persons the link between verbal and physical aggression should probably be weakened, which incidentally will go a long way toward accomplishing the third objective. Desensitization to fear of retaliation and to fear of losing control may also be helpful (see the Behavior Therapy section for this, too).

Reducing the individual's anger, the second goal, is not likely to be achieved by talking *about* various sources of annoyance, and a venting technique usually works best for this (see the Gestalt Therapy section of Chapter Four).

Before using either assertive training or emotional venting, the counselor should determine that the counselee can tolerate such procedures. Persons with only marginal contact with reality (e.g., borderline psychotics) and individuals who are extremely volatile are likely to worsen with any technique that further loosens up their cognitive (mental) controls.

Inadequate personality: Such a person is forever planning new ventures and scheming new schemes, but can never quite muster the wherewithal to see them through. He seems to lack the requisite physical and emotional stamina despite appearing neither intellectually nor physically deficient. His judgment is faulty, however, since his disastrous rate of success does not dissuade him from embarking on future enterprises, many of which border on the bizarre. For example, one such individual had unsuccessfully attempted one unsound venture after another, only to begin collecting used tires which he hoped to sell to a foreign country. He assembled large quantities of old tires on his front lawn until the police, upon neighbors' complaints, insisted on their removal. On mental examination, this man was not grossly out of touch with reality (not psychotic). Some inadequate persons are less inclined to initiate faulty schemes, but find it impossible to meet everyday life demands, particularly family responsibilities, whether economic or emotional. They are not especially hurtful, just insufficient. Such persons are usually compliant and are characteristically dependent.

The underlying personality dynamic of the inadequate personality is difficult to state in general terms. Some such persons are literally afraid of success and show a type of "promotion neurosis." Others are depressed and keep themselves energized by maneuvers they unconsciously do not intend to carry through. Still others enact a life role of repeated failure in order to elicit concern and support from relatives and friends.

Counseling should be aimed at gradually building self-esteem, increasing the individual's capacity to evaluate the soundness of his ventures, and fostering self-reliance and independence. The latter may be quite difficult, since these persons are fundamentally passive and dependent. They typically expect the counselor to solve problems and provide answers. To be of maximum benefit as a counselor to an inadequate person, it is best to avoid adopting either the role of sage or provider, since both of these implicitly foster inadequacy. The counselor should serve as a consultant, trying to maintain a certain distance from practical affairs. If the counselor gets trapped into doing social work to a significant extent, he should refer the person to someone else for counseling.

Suspicious personality: Suspicious persons are difficult to work with in counseling because they are continually on guard for discrepancies, ulterior motives, and hidden agendas. Of itself, such alertness is, at worst, an obstacle to counseling. The difficulty is that evils and insults are sometimes perceived where they do not exist, i.e., they are incorrectly attributed to the counselor. If these suspicions assume the exaggerated proportions of persecutory delusions (fixed bizarre beliefs), you are probably dealing with a psychotic disorder, and the person should be promptly referred to a psychiatrist or psychologist. But here we are discussing not a psychosis, but a personality style. Projection (attributing one's own motives, thoughts, and intentions to others) is thought to underlie the unwarranted suspiciousness, together with low self-esteem, such that the individual feels compelled to maintain constant vigilance to protect himself from even slight affronts, which are experienced as acutely painful. As might be expected, suspicious persons are chronically tense. They are also rigid and usually display an unrealistic sense of self-importance to bolster their faltering self-appreciation.

The primary goal of counseling should be to increase feelings of self-worth, helping the person value himself as he is rather than for what he feels he needs to be. But be careful not to alarm a suspicious person by being overly warm or friendly. Positive gestures that would comfort most people often prove distressing to suspicious personalities who cannot tolerate any form of emotional crowding. The best approach is a congenial but matter-of-fact one, without trying to move in too quickly or even to win confidence. Like trust, control is a central issue to suspicious persons. It is necessary to allow such a person the emotional distance he needs to feel he is in control. A difficulty that occasionally arises is that the counselee feels the counselor is violating his confidences or even taking sides against him. The counselor must be alert to this possibility and avoid situations that foster such projection. For example, it is usually risky to see the spouse (or anyone else involved) without the counselee present.

Countersocial personality: I am using the word "countersocial" in preference to "antisocial," the usual designation, because the latter term tends to be confused with what I have discussed above as seclusive. Countersocial persons are aggressively manipulative, and show little regard for others. They readily exploit people, experience conspicuously little guilt; and quickly dismiss challenges to their behavior with the flimsiest of rationalizations. Most countersocial personalities are charming, likeable, smooth . . . and coldhearted. They are typically good talkers, and frequently work at sales jobs where they find a use for their ruthlessness. Countersocial persons are relatively anxiety free, a characteristic that lends them social attractiveness, but they are often impulsive and fail to consider the consequences of their actions. While most personality neurotics live too little in the present, always thinking of the past or worrying about the future, these persons dwell almost exclusively in the now. They are quick to make promises but slow to keep them. Such individuals are emotionally superficial and do not maintain deep relationships. Their capacity for intimacy and love is severely limited. Clinicians sometimes designate them by the terms psychopathic, sociopathic, or criminal personality.

Countersocial persons are exceedingly difficult counseling prospects, but most clinicians find this out the hard way since such people are initially interesting and likeable. They can be vicious, however, and are unlikely to alter their basic exploitative orientation. In short, they are demanding, hurtful, self-centered, and callous. Countersocial persons are usually poor investments of counseling time, partly because they do not have the capacity to become sufficiently involved in counseling to benefit from it. Countersocial persons should probably be referred to a psychiatrist or clinical psychologist.

Perfectionistic personality: Perfectionistic persons are anxious and control their anxiety through compulsive defenses, i.e., by elaborately structuring their lives and environment. They are usually moralistic, rigid, controlling, and stubborn. Perfectionistic people are prone toward intellectualizing and have trouble experiencing emotions without clouding the air with all sorts of abstractions and philosophical speculations. They are supreme rationalists, clinging to dispassionate analysis as the solution to every problem. This serves to protect them from disturbing feelings in themselves. Such persons have a particular fondness for words and for making sure you understand exactly what they mean, even if it takes a great deal of unnecessary time. Many perfectionists are so "tight" that their ability to enjoy anything is sorely limited. In contrast to the countersocial personality, the perfectionist is overconcerned with responsibility and propriety. He is methodical, thorough, and thrifty to a fault. But mostly he is anxious and afraid. Like the suspicious person, he is worried about loss of control. He keeps close watch on his impulses lest they overwhelm and embarrass him. Reaction formation (unconscious thoughts and feelings being converted into their opposites upon entrance into consciousness) is characteristic.

For an excellent introduction on how best to work with perfectionistic persons, the reader can consult the late Harry Stack Sullivan's writings on obsessionalism. Sullivan was a well-known psychiatrist who emphasized interpersonal communication in psychotherapy. He speaks of the perfectionistic or obsessive person as trying his best to obscure his real meanings, despite his show of attempting to achieve perfect understanding. Sullivan would often say to his patients, when they began to obsess, that they were "bringing in the fog again." He points out the ability of such a person to get the therapist "stuck in flypaper" through all his clarifications, digressions, and detailed repetitions. In fact, words represent a kind of magic to perfectionistic people.

A person with deeply ingrained obsessive qualities is difficult to work with because he will avoid or "fail to understand" confrontations of his personal feelings. Persons whose perfectionism is less marked can sometimes be excellent counseling prospects because they have the ability to understand what is going on — they are usually intelligent — and will stick with counseling longer than many other individuals. It is best not to get caught up in intellectual discussions of any kind and to do everything possible to keep the counselee's anxiety at a minimum.

Affective personality: Affective persons are characterized by their intense and pervasive moodiness. They are almost always depressed or elated, or alternate between the two, and their moods are not readily attributable to external events. Biological predispositions probably play a more important role in this personality neurosis than in those previously described, but the extent of this contribution is unknown. On the other hand, some persons chronically employ mood states, particularly depression, as a way of manipulating others into gratifying their emotional needs. Depression can also be a manifestation of internal conflict, especially involving the expression of anger. Clinicians often regard elation as a means of warding off immobilizing depression, since the physical conditions underlying depression and elation are incompatible.

Affective personalities frequently appear for counseling because of family crisis or acute depression. The management of depression is, at best, a complicated matter (see the section on Depression and Suicide in Chapter Four). Besides assisting the individual through whatever crisis exists, the counselor should try to determine if moods serve either as manipulative devices or disguised representations of hostility. If so, later counseling can be oriented toward gradually pointing out the instrumental quality of the mood and/or helping the person learn to express his anger verbally rather than to turn it on himself.

Psychoses
Psychotic conditions are the most serious of the psychological disorders and are characterized by a severe breakdown in mental functioning (decompensation). Such persons have gross defects in reality testing and, consequently, speak and act strangely if not bizarrely. Psychosis is best viewed as a state of extreme personality disorganization, to which perhaps anyone could be driven under adverse enough circumstances. A small percentage of the population are psychotic all their lives; many persons have intermittent bouts with psychosis, but most of us never reach this state of profound disturbance. Psychoses can be functional or organic (see the section on Organic Disorders

later in this chapter). Functional psychoses are divided into two general categories, schizophrenia and manic-depressive disorders.

Schizophrenia: Schizophrenia is characterized by marked disturbances in *thought* processes, particularly autism (inability to distinguish fantasy from reality). Emotion (affect) is either conspicuously lacking or inappropriate to external circumstance, and the individual is often strikingly ambivalent about almost everything and everyone. Speech varies from mild disconnectedness (loose associations) to incoherence, and overt behavior shows a corresponding range from slight peculiarity to bizarreness and social impropriety. As in most psychoses, disorientation is common such that the individual frequently cannot give the day and date (disorientation with respect to time), say where he is (with respect to place), or even who he is (with respect to person). Judgment is faulty, often resulting in an inability to manage one's affairs. Misinterpretations of reality can include hallucinations (perceiving what is not there, usually hearing voices) and delusions (rigidly maintained bizarre beliefs, usually about one's importance to the world or persecution at the hands of others).

Persons who appear schizophrenic should be directed or taken to a psychiatrist, since hospitalization may be required and since psychiatric medication is almost invariably necessary. Acutely psychotic persons rarely profit from counseling. Most county hospitals have facilities where a psychiatric evaluation can be conducted.

Manic-depressive psychosis: Whereas schizophrenia is primarily a thought (cognition) disorder, this set of syndromes centers around a predominant and pronounced *mood,* either elation or depression. Occasionally, an individual will alternate between the two, but in any event, his moods do not seem directly related to environmental conditions. A manic person may run about frantically from place to place and activity to activity, and is unable to focus his attention for more than a few minutes. His speech is markedly accelerated (pressured speech) and he may even prove entertaining with his rapid barrage of quips and puns. Psychotically depressed persons, on the other hand, may not speak at all, and when they do, they usually demean themselves or talk of self-destruction. They are inactive, except for spells of crying, and will sit with head bowed for long periods. Some depressed persons show great anxiety and agitation, however. As with the manic individual, his moods are not easily attributed to circumstance. Manic-depressives should be provided with immediate psychiatric attention, especially since suicide is an ever present possibility. Hospitalization and medication are frequently required.

Schizo affective psychosis: This disorder reflects a mixture of schizoid and manic-depressive characteristics. Psychiatric management is necessary.

Stress Reactions
Stress disorders (transient situational disturbances) are abnormal mental states and behaviors, sometimes extreme, which occur in otherwise normal persons under conditions of environmental hardship. Events that might precipitate such a condition include military combat, college failure, or divorce. For a child, separation from a parent or moving to a new community could induce temporary disturbance. Older persons might react similarly to retirement, or to their children leaving home for school, marriage, or the armed services.

Persons manifesting stress (adjustment) reactions usually profit from supportive counseling, but the counselor or therapist should determine if a more longstanding disorder underlies the transient one. A brief evaluation by a clinical psychologist or psychiatrist can be helpful in making this determination. (See the section on Crisis Intervention in Chapter Four for further guidelines on helping persons who show stress reactions.)

Disorders of Aging
Problems associated with aging, especially among women, are well known to the public. "Change of life" symptoms — usually irritability, depression, and/or suspiciousness — have traditionally been considered direct consequences of

biological alterations accompanying, at least in females, cessation of menstruation. Expert opinion now, however, deemphasizes physical changes as causative factors in favor of the psychosocial stresses that attend growing old. Aging disorders are probably not so much reflective of endocrine imbalances as of emotional reactions to impending "senior citizenship."

Women who develop aging disturbances do so from the early forties to mid-fifties; such disturbances may last from a few months to many years. Menopause signals not only biological change but the decline of youthfulness as well. Since many women value themselves largely for sexual vivacity and attractiveness, markedly decreased self-esteem often goes hand-in-hand with this decline. Also, at about the same time, a woman loses another source of self-esteem, her role as mother. Children move out of the home for various reasons, leaving her essentially unemployed and feeling unneeded. This void is the backdrop for much anxiety and depression.

The psychodynamics of male aging reactions are similar, also centering around loss of self-esteem through role change. A man too faces sexual decline, specifically slowly decreasing potency, which can precipitate embarrassment if not severe humiliation, particularly in instances where his wife is notably younger, or demeaning. But perhaps even more stressful to an aging male is upcoming retirement, with its euphemized but clear message that he is no longer needed by society and that he is no longer to be entrusted with responsibility and its associated status. A gold watch and pension are meager replacements for a real job, however menial. Furthermore, money, another source of social influence, is usually sharply reduced. Onset of male aging reactions occurs from the mid-fifties to late sixties.

Some men, however, experience turmoil in their forties as a result of reevaluating the meaningfulness of their lives. Such a reassessment can be quite upsetting, and middle-aged men sometimes exhibit abrupt changes in lifestyle because of it.

Common to both sexes are increased sickness and debility, which threaten the aging person with helplessness, and on a deeper level stimulate fears of abandonment and aloneness. Fears of becoming dependent can prove overwhelming to persons who have functioned self-sufficiently most of their lives. And finally, impending death is the ultimate threat. Two sorts of aging reactions are common, depression ("involutional melancholia") and exaggerated suspiciousness. The probability of self-destruction, although low for the general population, is relatively high for older persons, particularly those lacking significant other people in their lives. Any older person who appears depressed or otherwise significantly disturbed should be referred for psychiatric or psychological evaluation. In most cases, the consulting clinician will recommend supportive counseling by the referring clergyman, but occasionally other measures, such as brief hospitalization, are necessary. Psychiatric medications, especially anti-depressants, are often needed.

Psychophysiological Symptoms

Psychophysical (psychosomatic) disorders involve real bodily disturbances which are brought on or exacerbated by emotional states, usually anxiety. Often the individual is unaware of the causative role of emotions in his condition. Examples include tension headaches, high blood pressure (hypertension), bronchial asthma, gastrointestinal ailments such as peptic ulcer, constipation, or "heartburn," and certain skin disorders. Note that the presence of one of these conditions does not necessarily imply a psychophysiological cause. A physician must decide whether such causation exists. For example, many cases of hypertension are caused by other physical ailments.

The management of psychophysiological disorders is best left to a psychiatric physician or internist, but counseling for other, perhaps underlying problems may help decrease the physical expression of psychological tension.

Chemical Dependencies

Drug dependence is largely a medical problem, but it is useful for the counselor to know something about the kinds of substances commonly abused. Opium derivatives (narcotics), such as heroin and morphine, are well known to the public as dangerous drugs, partly because most opiates are rarely if ever prescribed, i.e., they are strictly illegal. But another class of drugs, the barbiturates, are more sinister in that they are frequently given as sleeping pills, so that whereas opiates are usually obtained only by fringe members of society, barbiturates ("barbs" or "downers") pass through almost every medicine cabinet in the country at one time or another. Persons who become heavy barbiturate abusers characteristically have to be hospitalized and gradually withdrawn from the drug lest convulsions occur through abrupt termination. Most often abused of the barbiturates are Seconal (secobarbital, "Reds"), Amytal (amobarbital), and Nembutal (pentobarbital, "Yellow Jackets"). Barbiturates are responsible for many accidental fatalities because, unlike tranquilizers for example, the margin between prescribed and lethal dosage for sedatives is customarily narrow, and also because of strong potentiation effects (one chemical increasing the potency of another) with alcohol. Persons who routinely abuse barbiturates, however, build up a tolerance to the drug so that they are able to ingest larger and larger quantities as time goes on, amounts that in the beginning would perhaps have proved fatal. Both opiates and barbiturates are physiologically habit forming such that a whole range of systemic disorders follows abrupt cessation after prolonged use.

Before leaving the topic of barbiturates, a common danger accompanying use of these drugs at bedtime deserves mention. Since barbiturates produce what amounts to a temporary organic brain syndrome (see next section) marked by clouded consciousness, people who leave the drug bottle on their night table often wake up time after time during the night and repeat the dosage, forgetting that they have already ingested more than enough. Many persons have died because of this error.

Psychedelics are also used widely, though illegally. The mildest of these substances is marijuana ("grass" or "pot"). There is some question whether it should be classed as a psychedelic since its major effects seem to be euphoria and distorted time perception rather than serious sensory alterations. LSD ("acid"), mescaline, and psilocybin are the most commonly used of the powerful psychedelics. Probably the greatest danger associated with use of these chemicals is impaired judgment. Users occasionally do bizarre things such as walking into the path of a moving vehicle, believing themselves to be immortal. Like most chemicals, though, psychedelics are probably unlikely to precipitate these kinds of extreme behavior in persons who are not already quite disturbed. These substances are not nearly as well understood as the other drugs mentioned, but it appears that they do not produce physiological withdrawal disturbances. But the stronger hallucinogens like LSD sometimes produce curious symptoms known as "streaks" or "flashbacks" — the user repeatedly reliving a distressing experience which occurred under influence of the chemical ("bad trip" or "bummer"). Sometimes these flashbacks occur on and off for weeks or months.

Benzedrine ("bennies"), Dexedrine ("dexies"), and Methedrine ("speed") are amphetamines, often called "pep pills" or "uppers." They induce exhilaration and blissfulness, and while not leading to physiological withdrawal symptoms upon abrupt termination, they do foster a strong psychological dependence on repeated amphetamine use. Chronic use of these substances greatly stresses the body, particularly the cardiovascular system (heart and blood vessels).

Any person who appears to have clouded consciousness or to be exuberant or otherwise "out of it" ought to be questioned about drug usage. People abusing chemicals need medical evaluation and attention.

Alcoholism is also a chemical dependence but discussion of this widespread problem will be deferred to Chapter Four.

Organic Disorders

Organic Brain Syndromes

Many sorts of physical disorders can diffusely impair brain tissue, resulting in various psychological disturbances.

Among these disturbances are disorientation and mental confusion, memory difficulties (especially for recent events), impaired judgment, emotional superficiality, and generally reduced intellectual ability. Some organic brain syndromes (OBS's) are temporary while others are permanent. The psychological symptoms produced by some are severe enough to be termed psychotic, whereas those of others are not. Organic brain syndromes are medical disorders, requiring diagnosis by a physician, preferably a neurologist or psychiatrist.

Illustrative of physical conditions which can produce an OBS are alcoholism, certain dietary deficiencies, drug overdoses, poisoning, various endocrine or metabolic disorders, brain tumors, syphilis, some epileptic conditions, cerebral arteriosclerosis, general systemic infections such as malaria or typhoid fever, brain injuries, and various degenerative diseases of the central nervous system. Senility is also a kind of OBS.

Mental Retardation
About two percent of the population can be considered intellectually defective, and approximately another ten percent are marginally retarded. But intelligence test scores (IQ scores) are not fixed values and may vary as much as twenty points or more from testing to testing. People may appear to be brighter or duller at different times.

For statistical reasons, most IQ tests are set so that the average person gets a score of 100. An individual who is more intelligent than 85 percent of persons his age gets a score of about 115, and someone brighter than 95 percent of his age-mates gets a score of about 125. An IQ score of 140 would be obtained by only a few people out of a thousand. In the other direction, an IQ score of 85 suggests that the individual excels only about 15 percent of persons his age and a score of 75 indicates that the person's ability probably exceeds only 5 percent of the population his age. Scores below 60 are about as rare as those above 140.

Before mentioning some of the causes of mental retardation, I would like to make two related points. The first concerns the validity of traditional IQ tests and the nature of "intelligence" itself. Commonly used IQ tests are useful as predictors of intellectual performance within a typical middle-class environment, say a grade school. But they do not adequately measure other important aspects of cognitive functioning such as resourcefulness or creativity. In fact, since IQ tests largely measure acquired knowledge, which is obviously greatly determined by past opportunities for learning, they no doubt fail to measure the brilliance of many individuals whose educational experiences have been limited. Intelligence tests measure knowledge more than they do organic endowment.

The history of how men have viewed intelligence is fascinating, partly because of the opposing notions that have been maintained at different times. This history is too involved to be detailed here, but you may find it helpful to know that the prevailing idea of "general intelligence" is being called into serious question. Most of us have come to believe that a person is generally smart, not so generally smart, etc., based on the assumption that intelligence is one or at the most a few qualities. Some eminent psychologists are challenging this assumption, maintaining that there are more than a hundred kinds of intelligence, all more or less independent of one another.

The other issue I want to raise is a social one and concerns how retardation is viewed. Labels such as idiot, imbecile, and moron are no longer used by professionals because they do not aid clinical practice and only add to existing prejudice against intellectually handicapped people. So try to be aware of the social effects of the words you use in talking about retarded people, especially when speaking with relatives of such persons. Even the word "retarded" itself can be painful to a loved one.

Persons whose IQ scores fall between the low 50s to mid-60s are considered mildly retarded, and those whose scores are between the mid-30s and low 50s are regarded as moderately impaired. Below this a person is severely retarded and requires almost total custodial care.

Literally hundreds of specific physical abnormalities can

produce mental deficiency. To list some examples: congenital syphilis, congenital rubella (German measles), prenatal poisoning (carbon monoxide, lead, etc.), prenatal viral infection, mechanical injuries or suffocation (asphyxiation) at birth, various metabolic or nutritional diseases, brain tumors, and genetic defects (such as an extra chromosome of the twenty-first pair type which causes "Mongolism" or Down's syndrome). Despite the range of disorders which can produce mental defectiveness, it is not possible to specify the etiology in most cases. For all practical purposes, retardation cannot be cured, even though many retardates are educable or trainable.

Preview

In this chapter I have presented on overview of the various kinds of psychological disorders. This information will assist you in evaluating the nature and severity of the problems people bring to you, a task we will consider more extensively in Chapter Three. In the next chapter, I will deal with several different ways of conceptualizing counseling and will also discuss some of the qualities of effective counselors and of good helping relationships.

Recommended References

Coleman, J. C. *Abnormal Psychology and Modern Life,* 4th ed. Glenview, Ill.: Scott, Foresman and Company, 1972.

Coleman's text is probably more widely used than any other in Abnormal Psychology courses. It is lucid, comprehensive, and practical, but does not devote a great deal of space to reviewing theoretically oriented research, an advantage for non-psychologist readers.

(Hardcover; about $12)

Freedman, A. M., and H. I. Kaplan (Editors). *Comprehensive Textbook of Psychiatry.* Baltimore: The Williams and Wilkins Company, 1967.

This edited text is probably the best reference work available in the field. Most contributors are eminent researchers or practitioners in the area in which they write. It includes detailed coverage of the history of psychiatry, basic behavioral science, theories of personality and psychopathology, neurology, clinical assessment, forms of mental disorders, psychiatric and psychological treatment, child psychiatry, and community and social psychiatry. Over 1600 (large) pages, it is well worth its price. (Hardcover; about $25)

Hinsie, L., and R. J. Campbell. *Psychiatric Dictionary*, 4th ed. New York: Oxford University Press, 1970.

Although most clergymen would probably be hesitant to invest about $20 to purchase a psychiatric dictionary, this work is the best available. A much shorter dictionary is put out by the American Psychiatric Association (Washington, D. C.) entitled *A Psychiatric Glossary: The Meaning of Terms Frequently Used in Psychiatry*, 3rd ed., which sells for about $1 (Paperback).

Pfeiffer, E. *Disordered Behavior: Basic Concepts in Clinical Psychiatry*. New York: Oxford University Press, 1968.

This short book presents brief overviews of various disorders and treatments. It is a good, but inexpensive, introduction to traditional psychiatry. (Paperback; about $5)

Ullmann, L. P., and L. Krasner. *A Psychological Approach to Abnormal Behavior*. Englewood Cliffs, N. J.: Prentice-Hall, 1969.

This unorthodox text, written by two famous behaviorists, regards abnormal behavior as learned in the same way that normal behavior is acquired. Its posture is much different from more traditional books in which intrapsychic conflicts are considered the bases for abnormality. Ullmann and Krasner's book offers a view of psychopathology worth serious consideration and not adequately covered in most similar texts. (Hardcover; about $10)

CHAPTER II

DIMENSIONS OF COUNSELING

The Domains of Counseling and of Psychotherapy
Conceptions of Counseling
Features of the Counseling Interview
Qualities of Effective Counselors

HELPING ANOTHER PERSON with his psychological problems is often a taxing, somewhat bewildering, and anxiety-ridden enterprise. Human difficulties are rarely easy to ameliorate, so the clergyman who takes on counseling responsibilities is in for some frustration and hard work. In your efforts to assist others with their personal problems, it will prove valuable to be familiar with the various kinds of psychological and psychiatric procedures commonly used by mental health professionals. With this knowledge on hand, you will more easily be able to decide whether to work with a particular person yourself or, if the required service is outside your area of expertise, to help him find assistance elsewhere. This may substantially lessen the stress of your often being the first person consulted in a crisis. A clergyman is frequently called on to be a one-man diagnostic, treatment, and referral team, and consequently, the more you know about available professional services, the more effectively and efficiently you will be able to perform this demanding job.

In the last chapter, I surveyed the different psychological disorders so that you would be familiar with the kinds of problems you may have to confront. In this chapter I will discuss: (1) similarities and differences between counseling and psychotherapy; (2) alternate ways of conceptualizing helping relationships and the assumptions that underlie these conceptualizations; (3) important features of all counseling interviews; and (4) the personal qualities of an effective counselor.

The Domains of Counseling and of Psychotherapy

The terms "counseling" and "psychotherapy" are ambiguous insofar as each has been defined in many different ways and there is a good deal of overlap between the two sets of definitions. Beyond the vague and misleading impression that psychotherapy is a "heavier" process than counseling, most of us would be hard put to distinguish between the two. If pressed, even many professionals would fall back on a distinction grounded in credentials, i.e., psychotherapy (a "treatment") is what doctors do and counseling is what everyone else does. Or perhaps a distinction would be drawn in terms of the frequency and duration of sessions — psychotherapy is a long endeavor, involving from one to five visits per week, while counseling is a brief and less intense process. Still another distinction might be made in terms of who gets what. "Sick" people are given therapy and normal people are given counseling.

There is an important and more or less definable difference between counseling and psychotherapy but it only coincidentally relates to these sorts of issues. I will try to clarify the nature of this difference in the following sections. Before I do, however, I would like to emphasize that psychotherapy and counseling are points on a continuum and that where one draws the line between the two is largely an arbitrary matter. In discussing counseling and therapy, I will treat them as separate entities for the sake of exposition, but try to keep in mind that this is merely a convenience.

Psychotherapy

Psychotherapy, as I will define it, is the process of increasing a person's emotional capacity and self-sufficiency. This implies a relatively permanent modification of the personality, one to which an individual must grow. Since genuine growth usually takes time, so does the psychotherapeutic process. However, in rare instances growth occurs quickly. And so it is not frequency or duration of visits *per se* that characterizes psychotherapy but rather the emotional change it facilitates. Unless there is emotional growth, no

real therapy has taken place — regardless of how long the client or the therapist keeps at it.
A similar commentary applies to the credentials issue. The possession of a psychiatric or psychological degree is no guarantee of the highly specialized skills required to do good therapy. I would venture that some well-credentialed therapists are incapable of doing very much that is therapeutic, largely because of the close relationship that exists between one's own level of emotional maturity and one's ability to facilitate growth in others.
Neither is psychotherapy a medical cure to be given only to the "mentally ill." In Chapter One, I pointed out that an organic conception of most psychological problems is of doubtful validity and utility. Part of the rationale for my criticisms was that labelling some people "sick" tends to foster the misconception that there is a clear-cut difference between these people and "the rest of us." Such a dichotomy is glaringly false and obscures the fact that we fall somewhere on a continuum ranging from gross psychosocial incapacity to full personal functioning. I am not denying the importance of biological predispositions to the development of the more serious psychiatric disorders, but merely suggesting that the notion of psychotherapy as a special medical treatment, appropriate only for the sick, is false and misleading. Since psychotherapy is the process of facilitating emotional growth, anyone with potential for human growth could probably profit from it.
Most of us carry around a good many unresolved psychological conflicts, along with the unexpressed feelings associated with them. That is, we felt something at one time but, for one reason or another, blocked our own emotional expression. We needed to laugh, but held it back. We needed to cry, but we bit our lip. We were angry but pretended to be calm. We loved but were embarrassed to say it. And now we console ourselves by assuming that, by some mysterious process, time has alleviated our need to express these feelings. We become more and more blunted as more experiences of incomplete emotion accrue to our mental storehouse. And so we increasingly lose our ability

to respond fully in the present; we increasingly surrender
our humanity, our ability to sense and to feel.

To the extent that a person loses touch with his emotions, he is likely to live below his potential. He will be less
joyful, relate to other people less effectively, and work less
creatively. Insofar as an individual blocks himself, he
relinquishes his God-given freedom. Psychotherapy is the
process of removing these blocks, of skillfully providing
a person with the occasion and the resources to shed self-
inflicted obstacles, of nurturing human growth and freedom.

It takes specialized training, experience, and aptitude to
learn how to provide these occasions in such a way that the
individual experiences just the right amount of frustration
and support to enable him to grow. Furthermore, when
specific symptoms are evident, such as those discussed in
the last chapter, it takes a seasoned knowledge of psychodynamics to ensure the rendering of adequate service.
Although there are many alternative approaches to psychotherapy, it may be helpful to say something about how I
do this work. Printed below is a copy of an orientation
sheet I give to many of my clients when I begin to work
with them in therapy:

The following information may help you get your bear-
ings during the initial stages of our work.

(1) As we work together, try to get the feel of yourself
and how you structure the time and our relationship. Do not
try to change anything about yourself until you're fully
aware of how you are at present. This will take some time,
so see if you can relax and let yourself be.

(2) Psychological maturation means learning to stand on
your own two feet. So while you may find yourself depending on me in the beginning, our goal will be for you to
"come into yourself," to develop increased self-sufficiency.
This growth takes place through facing what you have
avoided, attending to what you have ignored, and owning
the parts of yourself you have disowned.

(3) I'll be concerned with helping you come to know
who you are rather than with helping you be something different. Growth starts with what really is, not with wishful
thinking. Your greatest resource and ally is your self, not the

self or selves you may want to become. I will try to help you discover how you prevent the growth of yourself. (4) Chatting with me *about* problems or people, in and of itself, will probably not help much in the long run. You will grow more from feeling than from talking, from contacting yourself than from depicting yourself, from experiencing than from editorializing, from expressing than from controlling. I will try to show you ways of unblocking yourself or, to put it differently, of making your talk count. (5) Try to view psychotherapy as a kind of education. Good education brings out what is within the student. You know more about yourself than I or anyone else will ever know, so regard me as your consultant rather than as a judge and final authority. Also, try to view growth as a lifelong process. You can come and go in therapy as you please and can return for more work at any time in your life you so desire. So try not to expect a seal of approval or a graduation certificate. Decisions about how often to come in and when to discontinue therapy are up to you.

Many of these statements require explanation and qualification, and I do not expect that the person with whom I am working will fully comply with or even understand all my suggestions. Nevertheless, I find it useful, depending on the client, to give him this information at the outset; but I avoid lengthy discussions of it, since these are usually ways to delay the real business at hand.

A good psychotherapist customarily avoids becoming involved in his client's practical affairs, in the interest of helping him develop increased personal adequacy and of keeping the therapeutic relationship free of diversionary complications.* If the person wants to talk about such things, the therapist will not ordinarily object but he will focus more on how the individual is expressing himself than on the content of what he is saying. Normally he will

---

*Exceptions might be made if a serious crisis were suddenly to confront the client or if the person were unable to manage his own affairs, such as an individual with chronic and severe psychiatric disturbance or an intellectually handicapped person. However, some professionals would say that therapy stops and counseling begins at the point of practical intervention.

not give his client advice, assume responsibility for what he does, or attempt to manage his life for him.

Counseling

An effective counselor, on the other hand, is expressly concerned with what the therapist avoids. He wants to guide and support the person in his handling of present practical difficulties. The counselor is interested in improving the person's ability to deal with external circumstance, specifically the circumstance that currently confronts him. Any long-range emotional growth is a fringe benefit. Whereas an individual's life may markedly change in reaction to switching jobs or separating from his spouse, his basic emotional capacities may not change much, a fact that reflects the difference between counseling and psychotherapy. The therapist frequently bypasses immediate practical concerns in order to facilitate lasting emotional growth, while the counselor squarely tackles these concerns, hoping to assist his client with concrete problems.

It is worth noting that many people are not ready to undertake psychotherapy because they are not yet able to assume responsibility for their lives or to give up the support of others. A sensitive clinician can usually tell rather quickly to what extent the person before him is a candidate for therapy or for counseling. Because of a pressing crisis, the individual may be more in need of skillful support and advice than of efforts to increase his self-sufficiency and emotional responsivity. If the person is severely distressed or disturbed, he may need immediate management by a psychiatrist and perhaps hospitalization as well. After such a person has stabilized, with or without the aid of psychiatric medication, he may then be ready to undertake psychotherapy or he may first need competent counseling.

Oftentimes the pastoral counselor finds himself doing much more than providing support or giving advice. Some people are clearly in need of psychiatric management or therapeutic assistance but are unwilling to entertain any recommendation that they consult a psychologist or psychiatrist. In these instances, the clergyman must either do what he can to help or leave the individual to his own devices. And so the pastoral counselor winds up doing what amounts to a mixture of counseling and psychotherapy — he finds himself in the misty area between the two. In my discussions of counseling, I have taken this into account and have tried to supply useful tips on how to function effectively in this challenging no-man's-land.

Conceptions of Counseling

For the rest of this book, I will use the term "counseling" rather broadly, as including to a greater or lesser extent many of the features of what is called psychotherapy. I would now like to summarize some of the more important ways in which counseling has been conceptualized. As will be quickly apparent, there is a great deal of diversity in these definitions.

Counseling as Value Change

Some people suffer psychologically or socially because they cling to pursuits that are counter to the welfare of themselves or others. For example, certain persons are continually winding up in trouble as a result of acting without regard for society's well-being and, correspondingly, for their own either, since such disregard usually elicits retaliatory punishment. These persons have failed to internalize a system of values which checks their abusive and exploitative impulses (see "Countersocial Personality" in Chapter One). Effective counseling with such people entails modifying their values to include a sense of conscience, and so one way of viewing counseling is that it is the systematic alteration of personal values.

Another, very different example of counseling as value change would be helping the individual who is so conscientious that he makes little provision for his own growth or happiness. This sort of person might engross himself so thoroughly in work or trivial avocations that he rigidifies his life and deprives himself of virtually all pleasure and joy. Counseling such a client might be viewed as an effort to realign his values so that he looks after his own welfare more and after minutiae or production less.

Perhaps the main limitation of viewing counseling in this manner is that it tends subtly to encourage judgmental moralism. However, most people who profit from counseling do modify their values, and these changes may be an important part of your work with any particular client.

Counseling as Cultivation of Natural Growth

Counseling can also be viewed as the nourishing of a natural tendency toward psychological maturation which presumably exists in all of us. Several eminent psychologists, including Carl Rogers and Abraham Maslow, have proposed that each person tends toward "self-actualization" (Maslow's term), and the counselor's job is to allow this innate positive orientation to operate by providing a conducive emotional atmosphere. Seen this way, counseling is similar to what I discussed earlier as psychotherapy, except that: I view the therapist's task as much more substantial than maintaining a favorable climate; I'm not sure that all people are innately growth oriented; and I believe that psychotherapy must be emotionally intense to be effective. I find it useful to think in this vein, to the extent that it helps me remember that my client is largely in control of what happens in counseling and that my job is to facilitate rather than to force.

Counseling as Temporary Support

This conceptualization parallels the narrow definition of counseling given in the first few pages of the chapter, i.e., counseling as crisis intervention and short-term support. Nothing more is attempted than getting the individual through his immediate emergency, and anyone under acute stress might profit from this kind of temporary assistance. Guidelines for providing crisis-oriented help are given in Chapter Four.

Counseling as Habit Change

This mode of counseling involves teaching someone specific behaviors and is akin to a new psychological specialty called behavior therapy. While traditional forms of psychological help focus on features of consciousness, such as anxiety level, mood, rationality, etc., behavior therapists attend almost exclusively to observable actions. While not denying that they alter internal states with their treatments, their concern is to teach people to behave more effectively. For any individual, this may mean some combination of the following: unlearning self-defeating or maladaptive behaviors; acquiring new desirable behaviors; learning to modulate the intensity of behaviors; and learning to make "appropriate" response, i.e., to match the right behavior with the right set of circumstances. Behavior therapists argue that good traditional psychotherapists do these things anyway, only not efficiently or explicitly. Most human problems can be cast in a behavioral framework. To give us several working examples, let's consider: (1) an exceptionally timid person; (2) someone extraordinarily afraid of heights; and (3) a suspicious person.

Someone who complains of timidity might be helped by being persuaded to practice speaking up for himself (see the section in Chapter Four on assertive training). Similarly, a person with altophobia (fear of heights) might be "desensitized" (again see Chapter Four) to high places by slowly ascending a long staircase or riding in an elevator. In both these examples, our aim is to alter a behavior — in this instance, avoidance responding, and in the other case, assertiveness. Even though internal states, such as fear or even panic, may be altered, our concern is with overt behavior.

Now let's consider our third example, a suspicious person. Two problems immediately arise: (1) the moral-ethical issue of whether or not you ought to change something about a person which he has not asked you to change (most suspicious people are unlikely to ask you to help them overcome suspiciousness); and (2) how to modify an attribute of consciousness which, in contrast to a behavior, is not directly observable.

Most behavior therapists would sidestep the first problem by claiming that *any* counselor faces it and that it involves a question of appropriate implementation rather than of technique; or they might say that, since we constantly alter other people's behavior inadvertently if not haphazardly anyway, we ought to do it in a manner that is clearly in their best interests, regardless of whether we have explicit permission. To the second challenge, the behaviorist is likely to respond by saying that it is not suspiciousness *per se* that one seeks to change but rather expressions of suspiciousness. We cannot observe suspiciousness, we can only note verbal or nonverbal behaviors which we assume reflect it. "So," the behavior therapist might maintain, "far from trying to alter consciousness, we are specifically changing behavior."

A number of knotty philosophical problems are inherent in this position. But by taking at least a soft behavioral stance, the counselor is forced to attend to the obvious, to what his client is doing. And so it fosters practicality and immediacy, and prevents the counselor from getting so wrapped up in psychodynamic theorizing that he misses the obvious.

Counseling as Affective Release

As mentioned previously, most people carry around unexpressed feelings and would profit from learning to let them go in a fashion that is not damaging to themselves or to others. Furthermore, such expressiveness is a prime feature of psychological well-being. Consider the person who has just lost a loved one but is unable to grieve. Or the individual who is furious with his spouse but holds it in. Or the person who is unable to enjoy life because he keeps himself tightly bound up in an emotional cocoon.

Venting emotions can be of great benefit to most counseling clients and the freedom for such expression is an important aspect of any good interpersonal relationship, counseling or otherwise. At the same time, some individuals cannot tolerate the emotional exposure that accompanies suddenly releasing pent-up feelings. They are frightened by the quick relinquishing of their controls and defenses and are likely either to flee the counseling relationship or to come apart at the seams. So it is necessary to use good judgment in applying techniques that rapidly loosen up tightly managed emotions. Chapter Four presents guidelines for doing this type of counseling.

Counseling as Reincorporation

In the first chapter I discussed ways in which people develop psychological problems, including incorporation of faulty parental models (see sections on "Faulty Parental Models" and "Self-Instruction and Self-Reinforcement").

Incorporation is taking into one's personality, in a hook, line and sinker manner, the attributes of another person The person is swallowed, so to speak, and remains an undigested part of the personality. Some counselors conceive their task to be "re-parenting" the client, i.e., providing him with a new "introject" to replace the faulty one he now possesses. Hence, the counselor tries to be the truly good parent, someone who is benevolent rather than hurtful, accepting rather than rejecting, and nurturing rather than withholding.

The problem with this, as I see it, is that psychological growth entails getting rid of introjects, not replacing them with better ones. An integrated person lives by his own senses and standards, not by the internalized senses and standards of someone else. Although he is obviously influenced by others, he reworks whatever he experiences so that it becomes a connected and personal part of him and not just an alien parcel. Psychological growth involves reworking these introjected parcels so that they come to "fit in." (Parenthetically, I believe the Godly person is one for whom holy values are an integral part of his being and not merely an unassimilated checklist.)

It does seem clear, however, that even the best therapy or counseling encourages some incorporation. The counselor *is* likely, to some extent, to be regarded as a parent, no matter what he does. And in fact, this may be quite important to the success of many counseling relationships (consider how much psychoanalysts make of this in their discussions of "transference"). Nevertheless, try to remember that anything that fosters long-term dependency is probably detrimental to your client and that one can never be the sought-for perfect parent anyway. So it is best to stick to being an expert consultant.

Counseling as Perceptual Shifts

Some people have trouble because they seem to look at things the wrong way. Perhaps they expect trouble where it doesn't exist, or they regard the glass as half empty rather than half full, and so on. These people need new glasses. They need to learn to evaluate their lives by a more rewarding frame of reference or perhaps just to do a lot less evaluating. At root, most psychologies are perceptually centered. They try to specify how man comes to view himself as he does, how he knows his world, and how he puts the two together.

Counseling can be directed toward providing a person with alternate ways of seeing. A person can be taught to hear how he judges himself and others, and perhaps also to do this more benignly. Or he can be taught to see himself and his world more clearly, accurately sensing the assets and limitations of himself and others. Probably all but the behavior therapies specifically involve changes of this sort. The point to realize is that what you do with your client may dramatically alter his quality of consciousness. You may indeed teach him to view the world with fresh eyes.

Counseling as Insight Acquisition

Perhaps the most widely held notion of what counseling entails comes from psychoanalysis, the psychotherapy system developed by Sigmund Freud. An overview of psychoanalysis might be helpful at this point. Psychoanalysis has come to mean a number of things: a theory of personality (id, ego, superego, psychosexual stages, defense mechanisms, etc.), a technique for studying psychological problems (free association), and a therapy for ameliorating those problems (interpretation). These three aspects of what is collectively known as psychoanalysis are more or less independent of each other, insofar as the effectiveness of one is not inexorably linked to either of the other two. As a theory of personality, psychoanalysis proffers fine insights into the human psyche, and Freud added a monumental dimension to psychology and psychiatry with his discoveries and ideas. Many of the concepts in psychoanalytic theory are ambiguous and some are downright farfetched, but most clinicians would agree that Freud and his colleagues have provided us with a great deal of psychological understanding into people, especially of the subtle ways people deny and distort reality. As a technique of clinical investigation, psychoanalysis is weaker. Although free association may yield valuable hypotheses about how specific disorders develop, the method cannot be trusted to validate these hypotheses as well — a point many psychoanalysts have yet to concede. A person in analysis is subject to a host of influences, such as his own needs, expectations, and beliefs and the wishes of the therapist, and it is virtually impossible to eliminate these kinds of biases.

As a therapy, psychoanalysis fares the worst. It has been criticized on grounds that it is at best a slow process which only the rich can afford. However true this may be, I think analysis is more justly faulted because, as traditionally practiced, it is an intellectual rather than an emotional therapy. That is, the analyst tries to help his analysand understand (gain "insight" into) his own mental workings ("psychodynamics"). People need to experience themselves more than they need to understand their dynamics. In fairness, I would like to add that many psychoanalysts know this quite well and do excellent therapeutic work. But the popular idea that good psychotherapy results in the ability on the part of the client to know precisely why he does what he does is misguided. To be useful, insight has to be fairly *concrete* and *affective*. The more removed it is from immediate reality, the less it will help. All insight is not equally beneficial, and the quest for psychological understanding can become just one more defensive avoidance of reality. But probably all good therapy engenders some insight as a natural by-product of "coming into oneself."

Counseling as Interpersonal Transaction Study

I am going to devote a relatively large section to this topic because it is extremely important. This mode of counseling derives from the work of two remarkable psychiatrists, Harry Stack Sullivan and Eric Berne. Sullivan, who did his major work several decades ago, is the father of the "Interpersonal Theory of Psychiatry." He regarded psychological problems as manifestations of difficulties in relating to other people. These difficulties are said to result from adverse experiences with significant people during the course of growing up, and are characterized by anxiety, the fundamental psychiatric malady. This anxiety, in turn, results in faulty interpersonal communication. The job of helping such a person, as Sullivan saw it, involves diminishing his anxiety and improving his ability to communicate with other people. Sullivan is famous for his statement that "It takes people to make people sick and it takes people to make people better." Of particular interest to us here is that Sullivan repeatedly urged therapists to pay attention to what the client does in the therapy situation, i.e. what he is trying to achieve in the transaction. Is he attempting to manipulate the therapist into praising or reassuring him? Is he trying to aggravate or provoke the therapist? Sabotage him? Seduce him? Con him? Sullivan believed these sorts of things, and not necessarily what the patient said, to be the important material in therapy. In fact, he suggested that whenever a client says *anything* to you, ask yourself what else he could possibly mean. It is hard to emphasize sufficiently the importance of this kind of awareness.

According to Sullivan, one of the best tools available to any counselor is his own gut-level intuition. Rather than focusing on what your client is saying, it is often best to attend to how *you* feel as he says it. Do you feel confused? Perhaps it is because the client is not speaking plainly, i.e., maybe he is confused. Do you feel anxious? Maybe you're picking it up from him. Do you feel distant? Unable to take hold interpersonally? It may be that your client is putting you off. Caution must naturally be exercised in coming to such conclusions in order to avoid projecting your reactions onto your counselee. But with experience, it is often possible to separate out your own psychological individuality from that of your client. So trust your intuition.

The other major impetus for studying how people relate to one another has been transactional analysis, the system formulated by Berne. This is a comparatively new form of therapy which centers around showing people how they set themselves and others up for trouble. People are said to function at any moment in one of three "ego states," parent, adult, or child; and Berne brilliantly shows what happens when people toss a curve into their interpersonal transactions, thus making them into "games." For example, if I offer to console (parent) you and then renounce you for your neediness, I am double-crossing you in the transaction. Such games are at times so serious that they can result in death, for example, the lifetime alcoholic or the bleeding ulcer patient. I strongly recommend that you become familiar with the work of both Sullivan and Berne (see the book by each recommended at the end of the chapter).

As a qualifying aside, I would also like to mention the adage that comes out of Gestalt therapy, developed by Fritz Perls. "You do unto others what you do to yourself." If this is true, limiting your counseling to the analysis of interpersonal transactions may never get to the root, *intra*personal problem.

Counseling as Sensory Awareness

A new form of personal help has recently emerged, that of reuniting an individual with his body and so with his physical senses. Most of this work is done in groups, whether called growth groups, encounter sessions, or whatever else. Since some of these groups are incompetently conducted, most professionals tend to close themselves to the core value that exists in the human growth and encounter movement.

The majority of professionals, in my opinion, pay far too little attention to the body, the physical repository of

psychological process. We regard the psychological as separate from the physical, and so miss the fact that how we
feel is reflected in our gait, in our posture, in our muscle
tone, and in our blood chemistry. Furthermore, we are
largely unaware that certain biological dysfunctions, such
as muscle tightness, can become so habitual that, even
under favorable psychological circumstances, the person
just cannot relax. A new wave of psychologists and physicians are carefully studying the interdependence of mind
and body, and are trying to reawaken the sensory capacities
of their clients.

Features of the Counseling Interview

Having summarized a number of different ways to con-
ceptualize counseling, I would now like to discuss some
important features of all counseling relationships. This material will provide a framework in which to fit the specific
techniques and procedures to be presented in Chapters
Three and Four.

The Client's Involvement

Some counseling relationships are so well handled that the
client eagerly explores his feelings, ideas, and attitudes,
and freely opens himself to hear what the counselor has to
say. The counselee actively pursues himself and, regardless
of coming face to face with disturbing material, on one
level he enjoys every minute of it. Other counseling relationships never come close to this. The client beats around
the bush or leads the counselor on wild goose chases, concerned more with self-protection than with learning or
growing. Although clients differ widely in their capacity
for self-disclosure and in their desire for change, how the
counselor handles an interview also has a lot to do with
how well it goes.

In Chapter Three, I will go over specific ways to conduct the kind of counseling session that is likely to encourage the client to immerse himself in the helping process.
Here I would merely like to highlight that good counseling

usually means good client involvement, the kind of involvement that allows him to concentrate on *his* psychological exploration and nearly to forget the presence of the counselor, even though resonating with him. Good counseling involves the dropping away of restrictive self-consciousness in favor of keen self-awareness. And this, I believe, happens only when the counselor does his job sensitively and expertly.

Structure and Who Leads Whom

In almost every kind of interpersonal relationship, subtle struggles for control and dominance emerge. Most of the time these struggles center around who's going to do the most talking or even who's going to do the least, but sometimes they take a more invidious form, such as battles for controlling rights in the life of one of the participants.

Any such conflict is categorically fatal to a counseling relationship. There is only one way to "win" this kind of struggle with a client and that is to give up the fight. Although some counselees require firm direction, you will rarely help someone you are trying to dominate, even if "it's for his own good." The counselee has to feel that you are not threatening his personal freedom and that you'll respect his human prerogatives. People are much more apt to heed what you say and imitate what you do if you have no vested interest in controlling or besting them.

So my second point is that the counselee is the person who ought to hold the controlling interest in your working relationship. Of course, you need to set certain limits for your own comfort and protection (such as at what time the interview begins and ends), but the client must retain control over what he does during the session.

Focus

In this section I would like to make a similar point but embellish it a bit. By and large, the client ought to determine what you do in counseling, as discussed in the preceding paragraph. At the same time, how you respond to what he says, which aspect you attend to, can have an im-

portant influence on the direction of the interview. For an
illustration, consider the following words spoken passion-
ately by a client:

> That's when I really got fed up with him and told him to
> get out. I just took his things, clothes and all, and threw
> them out the door. I screamed and yelled and threw things.
> And then the squad car rolled up to cool things.

To make the point dramatically, it would be inappropriate
and unfeeling to respond with "Did they arrest you?" or
even "What did he do when you threw his things out?"
Here is a person pouring out something that is personally
vital, and it is inept to focus on anything but affect. I might
say, "So you really pulled out all the stops and let yourself
fly" (rather than "let your rage fly," to indicate that the
rage is part of the person).

In general, it is better to attend to feelings than to facts
and to stick close to what the client has said. Notice that
in the foregoing example I focused on emotions rather than
on circumstances, and that I tried to capture the essence of
what the counselee had said. Statements that do this are
likely to prompt the client to stay with his feelings.

Blocking and Resistance

Two sorts of occurrences tend to interrupt the flow of
counseling. The first is the client freezing up, being unable
to talk, or having "nothing to say." Although these can be
instances of interpersonal resistance, which we will discuss
in a moment, they are usually manifestations of a psychological sore spot, of the client's getting "too close for comfort" to some unwanted feeling or attitude. Probably the
best way to deal with such blocking is merely to take note
of when it happens, i.e., what the client was talking about
just before he stiffened up. If he continues to block, there
are ways to try to help him out, and I will deal with some
of them in the next chapter.

Resistance — the second kind of interruption — has at
least a couple of meanings in psychology. It frequently
means the act of keeping from consciousness certain troublesome realizations. But it also refers to the client setting

himself against what the counselor is trying to accomplish. In actuality, these are two sides of the same coin since the counselor commonly attempts to bring the client to awareness of the very material he seeks to avoid. The skillful management of resistance is central to good psychological work. See Chapter Three for guidelines on handling resistance.

Explicitness of Goals

Goals in counseling can be explicit, implicit, or nonexistent. That is, what you and the counselee are trying to do can be openly stated, known but not declared, or it can evolve as counseling proceeds. Furthermore, goals may be clear to one person, say the counselor, but vague or unknown to the other.

To the extent that it is possible, counseling objectives should be out in the open. The client may not be able to understand everything you might visualize as a goal in working with him, but he ought to have a pretty good general idea of what you're trying to do. One advantage of maintaining and continually updating clear goals is that it helps keep the counselor and the counselee on the track, even if this track is a broad one. If you have no aims as you work with a particular client, you're probably chatting with him — which is fine so long as you both know you're doing it.

The Issue of Responsibility

Helping relationships also differ with respect to how the responsibility for the counselee's life is divided between the client and the counselor. The amount of responsibility a counselor ought to assume is one of the most crucial and hotly debated issues in psychology. Some practitioners maintain that they are the experts and that they must correspondingly manage the lives of their counselees, very much as a general physician would do for his patients. Others take a more moderate stance and hold that the clinician need not bear the whole burden of responsibility but that he certainly must carry a significant part of it. Still others adamantly refuse to accept any responsibility for their clients' lives and steadfastly reject the management

duties implied in the doctor-patient role model. I believe
there is no blanket rule for deciding the optimal division of
responsibility for all counseling relationships. How much
direction and management a counselor should offer largely
depends on the individual client. Unfortunately, the term "responsibility" is used to mean
two very different things. There is a fine but immensely
important line separating healthy concern from a neurotic
need to control. It is possible to care a great deal about
people without needing them to be different — even if they
are in terrible straits and even if you see exactly how they
could change all that.* In general, *to the extent that you
are personally invested in changing your client's life, you
will make yourself miserable and do your job less effectively;* to this extent, you will be dependent on him and
subject both to the vicissitudes of his life and to his manipulation. In addition, he will probably sense your need to
control him — and that's bad news!

The less able an individual is to run his own life, the
more management and direction he will need. The worse
off your client, the more you'll have to do for him, sometimes even to the point of taking him by the arm and
bringing him to a hospital. But accepting this kind of
management responsibility — a manifestation of competent
concern — is entirely different from a compulsive need to
"see that things go right." It is important to recognize that
management is a type of support and that the more you
support an able person, the less he will learn the art of
self-support. So try using these guidelines: (1) "Care" as
much as you naturally do, bearing in mind that expressions
of concern are intrinsically supportive and that, therefore,
they may not be good for a particular client if dispensed
too liberally; (2) avoid "neurotic responsibility," the kind
based on your needs rather than on the client's; and
(3) manage a person's life only to the extent that he cannot manage it himself.

---

*For an excellent glimpse of what I am talking about, see the dialog
between the Lady and Frank, the Tragedian-Dwarf Ghost, in the latter
part of C. S. Lewis' *The Great Divorce.*

Qualities of Effective Counselors

The personal characteristics of an effective counselor are difficult to summarize, but psychological research has pointed to three qualities as being centrally important. I would like to discuss these qualities and then mention an additional one which I consider vital.

The Importance of the Counselor's Personality

Counseling cannot be reduced to a set of axioms because: (1) no one has ever come close to setting down the vast number of rules such a project would require; (2) a counselor could not possibly keep them all in mind at the same time anyway; and (3) treating a person according to canned rules is the very antithesis of what he needs. People who come to you for counseling need to experience you as honest, spontaneous, and "fully there." So how you feel and act as you work with a particular counselee is causally related to how much you're likely to help him.

Quality I: Empathy

The ability to feel with your client, to sense where he is psychologically, is very important. Although this may sound easy to do, it is often difficult to "read" your client correctly. In the interests of what people experience as self-protection, they frequently camouflage their real feelings and attitudes, and as a counselor you have to be sensitive enough to pick up the message behind the words. This implies "staying with your client," attending to how he speaks, the way he moves, the progression of his ideas, his facial expressions, etc.

Quality II: Warmth

Secondly, you must be able to convey concern without control, interest without pressure, warmth without manipulation. It is necessary to let your client know that you care about him but that you do this without smothering or crowding him. Empathy involves understanding and warmth has to do with affection. But these are integrally related, because you're not likely to show your client one without the other.

Quality III: Credibility

This attribute goes under the names of genuineness, authenticity, and congruence, the latter meaning that the counselor's words match his behavior and that both correspond to his feelings. If your client perceives that you are "saying nice things to him," he is not likely to trust you, and trust is the *sine qua non* of good counseling. A serious mistake many counselors make is to sacrifice their credibility in an attempt to be warm, caring, and accepting. They "try" to be concerned. No one ever communicated genuine concern by trying to work himself into it — if you don't feel it, don't say it.

A Postscript: Quality IV

In my opinion there is another quality necessary for effective counseling, and this is the ability to modulate the intensity of what you say and do. A sensitive counselor adjusts the forcefulness of what he says so that it's powerful enough to make an impression but gentle enough not to frighten or constrict his client. To do your job well, you must modulate the strength of your statements to match your client's tolerance for confrontation, without compromising the truthfulness of your reactions (no easy task!). Keep in mind that most counselors err on the side of diluting their words with meaningless insulation; they are too tactful rather than too blunt.

Preview

In Chapter One I discussed the different psychological disorders and in this chapter surveyed various ways of looking at counseling and counselors. Chapter Three will deal with the actual procedures one uses in trying to help another person in counseling.

Recommended References

Berne, E. *Games People Play*. New York: Doubleday, 1964.
    This short book is a gold mine of psychological insight.
Berne has catalogued many of the destructive ways in which people interact and has analyzed these interactions with

clarity and brilliance. I strongly recommend this work to you.   (Hardcover, about $5; also available in inexpensive paperback)

Bugental, J. F. T. *Psychological Interviewing*, revised ed. Los Angeles: Psychological Service Associates, 1966. This manual is a highly useful guide on how to conduct many types of interviews, including the counseling session. Bugental presents excellent material on some essential dimensions of psychological interviews and gives a host of examples which demonstrate the principles discussed.

(Paperback, about $7)

Sullivan, H. S. *The Psychiatric Interview.* New York: W. W. Norton, 1954. Sullivan offers many practical tips on the psychiatric interview, most of which are equally applicable to counseling. He deals extensively with both anxiety and communication, and gives pointers on various aspects of psychological interviewing.   (Paperback, about $3)

CHAPTER III

COUNSELING PROCEDURES

Initial Assessment of the Client
Structuring the Counseling Relationship
Basic Interviewing Techniques

IN THE LAST CHAPTER, I reviewed different ways of conceptualizing the counseling process and also discussed some basic dimensions of all psychological interviews. Finally, I summarized various characteristics of effective counselors and of good counseling relationships. We will now consider what one actually does to help another person psychologically. Whereas Chapter Two is primarily theoretical and, as such, contains many abstractions of the concrete realities of counseling, the present chapter is more procedural and applied. It is intended to flesh out the skeleton presented in the previous chapter, and includes sections on psychological assessment, structuring a counseling relationship, and basic counseling strategies.

Initial Assessment of the Client

When a counselor is asked to work with a person, the first thing he has to do is evaluate the general nature of this person's troubles. The better he can do this kind of assessment, the more effective he is likely to be as a helping agent.

Assessment Necessary and Inevitable

At one time in psychology, there was a heated controversy over whether or not one ought to categorize people and their problems. Some practitioners held that to do so was to oversimplify the complexity of human struggle and to restrict the clinician's range of vision so that he saw only those qualities in his client that conformed to his diagnosis. Other professionals believed that accurate evaluation and categorization was essential to effective treatment and approached the whole business with ritualistic thoroughness,

often engaging in trivial disputes over *the* correct label for
a person. As is common with such polar controversies, the
best position and course of action falls between the two
extremes. While the idea of perfect diagnosis in psychiatry
and psychology is largely a myth (see Chapter One), it is
important to recognize the general nature of the individual's
disorder — for example, whether he is chronically psychotic
or just acutely upset. And there is no acceptable way to
dodge this issue. It makes a great deal of difference, both
to you and the client, whether you consider him in need
of immediate psychiatric evaluation or of short-term supportive counseling. Whether or not you use diagnostic
terminology, you have to make a certain number of fundamental clinical decisions.

Preliminary Evaluation
The first kind of assessment you have to do when you see
a client is to evaluate his overall level of psychological
functioning. A seasoned counselor can accomplish this both
quickly and unobtrusively, without fanfare or undue for-
mality. The ability to blend assessment smoothly into your
initial interview will develop with practice.

Orientation for time, place, and person: Of primary
interest is how well in touch with reality your client appears
to be. Does he know the day of the week and the date?
Does he know where he is and how he got there? And,
finally, does he know who he is and who you are? Most
people have no difficulty supplying this information and
are therefore said to be "precisely oriented." If, on the
other hand, the client cannot correctly answer any of these
questions, you should suspect a serious mental disorder.
Sometimes "normal" people have to pause a moment to
figure out the date, but they have no trouble whatsoever
furnishing the other data. A person who looks confused
when asked for time-place-person information, or who cannot provide it, may be suffering from a severe psychiatric
abnormality, perhaps an organic or functional psychosis.
For example, schizophrenic persons or individuals under
the influence of psychedelic drugs may be disoriented in

one or more of these three spheres. Such persons should be taken for psychiatric evaluation if possible.

Ideational content and flow of ideas: A person's speech is an excellent clue to his psychological makeup. Both what he says and how he says it are revealing, not only of his stability, but also of his psychological style and orientation — what clinicians have termed "character structure."

A dramatic illustration of how psychological dysfunction may be reflected in speech disturbance is the "word salad" associated with certain forms of schizophrenia, for example, "no, no, not, cot, rot . . . there it is . . . the man in the moon . . . oh boy, toy . . . time, time, chime, chime." Less severe speech disturbances also exist, and in fact each person has a unique way of talking, even aside from voice inflections and the like. What an individual says represents a kind of psychological fingerprint, from which the tuned ear can discern much useful information. To elaborate on this just a bit: Does a person speak slowly and rigidly? Does his speech sound pressured and machine gun-like? What does he talk about — morbid and gruesome things which suggest turmoil and disorganization? Is he self-recriminating or does he blame his troubles on others? Do his statements follow one another logically or do you find yourself wondering how he got from one idea to the next? Thus, you can glean a good deal from speech if you listen attentively. Many of the qualities discussed below are assessed largely from the individual's use of language.

Intensity, range, and appropriateness of emotion: Since emotions are central to psychological functioning, evaluating a person's affect is crucial to good assessment. Does the person express his feelings or is he emotionally flat? Can he experience both joy and sadness, or is his emotional life bland and constricted, giving the impression of monotone grayness? Are his moods predominantly negative and depressive or, alternatively, is he on cloud nine and unable to come down? Are his emotional responses appropriate, or does he react in ways that seem grossly discordant with existing circumstance? Well-integrated persons show the capacity to experience a wide range of feelings, which generally seem understandable, while very disturbed persons are either zombie-like in their affective flatness, emotionally inappropriate, or profoundly elated or depressed. *Clarity of consciousness:* Noticeable blurring or clouding of consciousness is a concomitant of most serious mental disorders. Although it is possible for someone to be severely disturbed and not show clouded consciousness (some paranoid schizophrenics, for example), anyone with pronounced mental confusion can be assumed to be seriously disorganized. The actual problem may be anything from an organic syndrome to a functional psychosis.

Judgment and self-insight: Can the person make reasonable decisions on his own or does he need outside supervision and management? Poor judgment frequently leads to inappropriate behavior, some of which can prove dangerous to the individual or to others. An example of poor judgment resulting in tragedy was the college student some years ago who reportedly, while high on LSD, rode his motorbike into an oncoming train to demonstrate his invincibility. An individual whose judgment is defective needs special care and ought to be examined by a psychiatrist or a psychologist.

A related matter is whether or not the person is aware of his problems and what they signify. I find that a good way to evaluate this kind of insight is to ask, "Who thought it would be a good idea for you to talk with me?" If the person says that it was someone else's idea, I then ask what was happening to prompt this. If he says it was his own idea to see me, I inquire about what led him to make the decision *at this time.* Through a few such routine questions, I can usually assess the individual's level of self-insight fairly quickly, and gather other helpful information in the bargain.

Overall impression: Finally, I try to get the feel of my client as a person by attempting to fit the pieces of information together, in my mind, so that they gel into a coherent picture. It is hard to specify all that goes into making such a judgment, but I can at least say that I pay careful attention to *what I feel* as I talk with the person.

Your own "guts," while not infallible, are one of your best assessment instruments.

Whom to Refer

One of the most difficult questions any professional must face is when to provide services and when to refer the individual to someone else. Probably the best rule of thumb for deciding this is to follow your instincts and heed the limits of your own competence. While you will have to develop your own set of decision rules on this matter, the following guidelines may prove helpful:

(1) Do not begin an extended counseling relationship with anyone who appears acutely psychotic, unless he has first been examined by a psychiatrist or psychologist. Such persons may require medication and/or hospitalization and should be taken, if possible, to a psychiatric physician. Give immediate support to anybody who needs it, provided this does not endanger your safety (most psychotic persons are not dangerous, even though their bizarre behavior can frighten even an experienced clinician); but do not begin long-term work with a person who seems seriously disturbed until that person has been checked over by someone intimately familiar with psychopathology. If the individual refuses to see a psychiatrist — and this commonly happens — you must use your own discretion as to whether to counsel the person or not . . . a difficult decision at best!

(2) Work with persons complaining of psychophysiological ailments (such as tension headaches, ulcers, etc.) only after they have consulted a physician. One reason for this recommendation is that the manifest ailment may be masking a more serious one.

(3) Someone showing neurotic symptoms should usually be evaluated by a psychologist. This is particularly important for persons with phobias, obsessions, or compulsions. The psychologist may recommend that you work with the individual or he may advise you to refer him to someone else. If you feel comfortable with the idea, you may want to try using the appropriate behavior modification technique (see Chapter Four), but this can be tricky.

Some people who appear at first glance to have only a symptom neurosis turn out to be much more disturbed. Many people adamantly refuse to consult a psychologist or psychiatrist but are quite willing to work with their clergyman. In these instances, one has little choice but to do his best under the circumstances. If you regularly talk with a psychological or psychiatric consultant, he may be able to advise you in such cases.

(4) Refer to a physician anyone who shows signs of possible neurological disease. Examples of neurological danger signals are: unusually intense or recurring headaches; visual abnormalities such as double vision or tunnel vision (loss of sight to the sides of the visual field); unusual movements of any kind including shaking, spasms, loss of coordination, and walking difficulties; certain language problems such as an inability to understand the spoken or printed word, inability to name common objects, and slurred speech; and significant pain, tingling, or numbness in any part of the body. Many times these symptoms appear in the absence of neurological anomaly, but it is better to be safe than sorry. When in doubt, consult a physician.

Structuring the Counseling Relationship

Getting Off to a Good Start

The first few minutes you spend with a client are very important, since the quality of these moments will set the tone for everything else you do. Even if you already know someone very well, the way you relate to him in this new role can profoundly influence the outcome of your helping effort, for better or worse. It is usually best to start off business-like, thereby communicating to the client that you do not minimize his difficulties, that you earnestly desire to help, and that you appreciate how opening oneself to another person can be both taxing and threatening. Taking your job seriously, by the way, does not mean acting morose or inordinately formal. It mostly means attending carefully and not talking frivolously. The initial few minutes will form a lasting memory for your client and, consequently, if you do your work well at the outset, you'll have built a solid foundation for your entire working relationship.

Background Information

I spend most of the first session gathering background information. This accomplishes a number of things. It allows me to get a sense of who my client is and of how he developed his difficulties. It also helps me assess his assets and limitations, points I might otherwise miss. Furthermore, my client begins to trust me by virtue of my concern and thoroughness, and he also starts to trust himself in the relationship. By observing the continuity to his life, that it has been a series of related trends and events, he becomes more accepting of his problems. He sees that they have their origins and, to that extent, is less inclined to deride himself for having them. Normally, I do not encourage people to search for causes because this usually fosters intellectualization and avoidance; rather, I try to connect them with what exists in the present. But during the first session or two, I am the one looking for reasons; and if my client develops a sense of self-acceptance out of this, so much the better.

In general, try to obtain at least the following information during your initial interview: (1) the person's full name, address, phone number, and place of work; (2) the problems leading him to seek help; (3) his marital status and, if married, number of children, spouse's name, and whether or not this is a first marriage for both parties; (4) his childhood history, including birth order, unusual events (such as the death of a family member or a serious childhood disease), and descriptions of his parents; (5) his adolescent history, along the same lines, with particular attention to significant friendships and dating history; (6) employment and military service histories; and (7) what he considers his major strengths and weaknesses.

Some psychologists use a standard form which they ask the client to complete before the first interview. You can easily construct such a questionnaire if you think it would be helpful; or else simply ask the person to chronicle his life, i.e., to list significant events, in order of occurrence, along with his age for each. But be flexible. Don't let such forms obscure your real purpose, to help your client. If a person seems unwilling to reveal himself on paper, put the questionnaire aside.

Explicit Statements of Problems and Goals

It is wise to obtain a clear statement of the person's problems and goals at the beginning of counseling. If you do this, the client no longer has to worry about whether or not to tell you about some of his most bothersome concerns. Often a person in crisis is highly motivated to disclose information about himself to the counselor. But as the crisis passes, he becomes more reticent to volunteer such material, and the week, say, between the first and second counseling sessions can be just enough to cool off his desire to open himself up to you. So get it straight at the outset. Find out exactly what your client's problems are and don't be afraid to ask personal questions. I sometimes ask the client to write down this information and I keep it handy for future reference and review. It is good to be explicit about your goals all through counseling. You don't have to make it a separate part of every session, but *you* ought to know what you're trying to accomplish and, as much as possible, your client ought to know too.

What to Accomplish in the First Session

You should accomplish at least three things in the initial interview: (1) obtain a clear picture of the person's problems and get some sense of how these relate to his lifelong development; (2) assess his overall level of psychological functioning and make a tentative decision about the kind of help he needs; and (3) if you are the person who is going to work with him, map out an agreement covering what you will be doing with him, i.e., formalize your mutual goals and set the terms of your relationship — for example, you guarantee the confidentiality of what he tells you and he agrees to notify you in advance if he cannot keep an appointment, etc. It is important to structure the relationship clearly, even if you do this implicitly, so that you will not have unnecessary misunderstandings later. You are making an informal contract and both of you need to know your privileges and responsibilities.

More Direct Openings

Some clinicians do not bother with history gathering or the other preliminaries I've recommended, and this sort of casualness is becoming increasingly popular. Some psychotherapists, for example, start the first session with "What brings you here today?" and take it from there. I do not advise this, however, because it takes an experienced professional to be able to afford the loss of information this entails. At the same time, don't let your desire to gather background material deaden your awareness of the human person who sits before you. His welfare is more important than the details of his history; when the two conflict, opt for the former.

The Physical Setting

The environment in which you do your work can significantly influence how well it will go. Try to be cognizant of the possible effects of the setting on your counseling, and be aware that different people are differentially sensitive to such effects.

The room: Keep your office or wherever else you do counseling at least reasonably neat. A disheveled room implies disorganization and lack of interest — it makes it look like you're so involved in other pursuits that you are not committed to your counseling. Beyond this, an orderly room has a calming effect on most people.

Aids: You ought to have comfortable chairs for both you and the client, and it is also a good idea to have a box of tissues at hand. A way to shut your phone off so that it does not interrupt your conversation is also desirable, since intrusive phone calls tend to annoy most clients and disrupt the counseling transaction.

How Frequently to Schedule Appointments

There are no fixed rules for deciding how often to see a particular person, but most clinicians use one meeting per week as a baseline and move up or down from there. A person is most amenable to change when he is upset, so you might want to work with someone in crisis several times the first week and cut down the frequency of visits as you progress. Although this format usually presents no problem to a clinician who charges a direct fee for his time, clergymen who counsel as part of their pastoral duties run the risk of the person resenting the subsequent reduction in counseling time. But I think this is a small risk and well worth taking. After doing this kind of scheduling for a while, most counselors are able to sense which people are prone toward tenacious dependency and, with these persons, define the limits of their commitment well in advance.

How to Manage Phone Contacts

Many clergymen spend their free evenings on the phone with counselees, often to the distress of themselves and their families. Much of this is unnecessary. There are always legitimate crises to which any counselor must immediately respond, but if allowed to, some people become insatiably dependent on a counselor to both his detriment and their own. Good counseling teaches people to stand on their own two feet, and your being available at all times for support tends to undermine the client's learning self-support. So place limits on your accessibility for all but seriously disturbed persons. Avoid reinforcing people for calling you at home by not becoming involved over the phone. Say immediately, for example, "I'd like to discuss this with you in person. Could you stop by tomorrow at 11:00?" If the time you suggest is not suitable, offer another. Most people who really need help will make it their business to adjust their schedules to accommodate yours. For the majority of clients, this extra hour can replace the next regularly scheduled appointment.

But be careful not to become too inflexible in your response to unexpected phone calls. For obvious reasons, you must distinguish between a person in serious crisis, who needs on-the-spot attention, and the clinging individual who does not contain his demands.

What to Make of Social Overtures

Some counselees will extend social invitations to you, such as asking you to dinner at their home. These are sometimes gestures of pure good will, but other times they are efforts to dilute counseling. Once they are tired of working psychologically, some people try to transform the counseling relationship into a social one rather than tell the counselor that they are bored, emotionally fatigued, or whatever. If this is the case, it is best to make it explicit for discussion rather than to go along with the social gambit and thereby reinforce indirect and manipulative behavior. Sometimes people resent the one-down position of the counselee role and try to socialize with the counselor to alleviate their discomfort. In this instance, there may be no harm and even some benefit to accepting the invitation. The important thing is that you think through the implications of your reply. It is difficult to decline invitations in a way that does not leave the client feeling rejected, and I have experienced many an awkward moment because of this. Nonetheless, I have found it best for me to be conservative in my response to social overtures. You may find a casual orientation most effective, and you may have to try several different stances until you find the one that is best for you in your work.

Individual or Marriage Counseling

A sticky question that frequently arises is whether both parties in a marriage should be seen jointly or whether one or both should be counseled individually. Again there is no pat answer. If you see both persons together, you tend to minimize the hazard that one will play you off against the other, by asserting, for example, that you feel he or she is right and that you agree the other person is responsible for all the trouble. You also guard against projection by the absent party, who does not have to guess about what you might have said about him since he was there. Finally, you make it unlikely that one member of a marriage will psychologically outgrow the other. On the other hand, seeing both persons together tends to foster both evasion of

responsibility and repetition of the same script they have
played out for months or years: both people naturally tend
to view their problems as "mutual," by which they mean
the other person caused them; and they tend to repeat the
same things they have said all along, although a sharp
counselor can take this very fact for therapeutic mileage.

Early Terminations in Counseling

People frequently show what has been called "hello-
goodbye" behavior in counseling. That is, they quickly
respond to support and terminate counseling before the
counselor has a chance to do much for them. Such "flights
into health," as psychiatrists call them, should be treated
as interruptions rather than as terminations. This will make
it much easier for your client to resume counseling later
on, insofar as he does not have to "swallow his words" or
"come back with his tail between his legs." His further
continuing of counseling is then just the natural picking up
of where he left off rather than an admission of previous
faulty judgment.

If, in your opinion, one of your clients is leaving counseling prematurely, try to convey to him that you accept
his decision to stop but that you will be available to carry
on your work if and when he wants to do so. In this way,
you will communicate that you respect his freedom of
choice but that you interpret his behavior differently than
he does. Do not pressure anyone into continuing, because
this will invariably lead to resentment. Furthermore, by
pressuring him you are giving the person good reason either
not to trust you or not to assume responsibility for his
choices. In almost every instance, you will do well to wait
out your client's reluctance and to recognize that each
counselee has his own sense of timing and rhythm for personal growth, patterns it is usually wise to accommodate.

I do, however, try to build in one safeguard against
abrupt termination (which may occur, for example, because the client is angry with me but wants to avoid telling
me so). I ask the person to agree at the outset to come in
at least once more after he has notified me of his intent to

discontinue. Such an "additional session option" helps prevent impulsive terminations, which are not good for the client and which are both jarring and baffling to the counselor. I think it's a fairly good rule of thumb to assume that sudden endings mask a hidden agenda.

A related issue concerns the point at which counseling is rightfully finished. Unless your goals are unusually circumscribed and behavioral, it is hard to judge to what extent they have been attained. I customarily respect my client's opinions on this matter but strongly encourage a gradual reduction in frequency of visits rather than an abrupt termination. One could argue for continuing work with a person indefinitely, on the premise that there will always be something to do — after all, nobody's perfect. But eventually you get to a point of diminishing returns, where the gains of going on do not outweigh the losses to the client's autonomy and self-sufficiency which are built into the counselee role.

Still another problem is how to taper off contacts with a clinging person. Some people are determined to hold on for what they feel to be dear life and regard efforts to facilitate their independence as punitive and rejecting. Often you will be able to sense in advance that someone is likely to be tenacious and you can discuss the importance of autonomy building. Thus you will already have laid the groundwork for effectively dealing with a difficult termination. When such a person balks at your decreasing the frequency of counseling sessions, you can point out where else in the person's life this sort of difficulty has come up. Even if your client does not acknowledge the validity of what you are saying, it will probably be beneficial to say it anyway.

The important thing is that your client not have a legitimate complaint, i.e., that you are not breaking an implicit agreement. Needy, dependent people are often skillful at getting an unwary counselor to promise unending concern, involvement, and, by implication, time. In doing this they invite rejection, since no counselor can be unlimitedly concerned and accessible. Even if true, statements such as

"No one else ever understood before . . ." or "I've been
so hurt by people letting me down, but you're different . . ."
ought to signal you to watch out for unexpressed demands
and expectations.

The Use of Consultants

In this section I would like to discuss the intelligent use
of various kinds of consultants. You will find that maintaining consultative relationships with certain secular professionals can be of substantial benefit to you in your
ministerial counseling. This is so because it gives you access
to a wide range of expert advice and also provides you with
pre-established referral channels, a major asset when you
have to take immediate action during a crisis.

How psychiatrists can help: Psychiatrists are the professionals best able to help you with persons who show
extreme mental disturbance (psychosis). Such persons often
need careful supervision as well as psychiatric hospitalization and/or medication. As a physician, the psychiatrist
can provide these services and can also assume major management responsibility for the person. In addition, the
psychiatrist is attuned to physical pathology and may catch
a somatic problem that another mental health professional might miss.

How psychologists can help: The title of psychologist is
much less precise than that of psychiatrist, but many states
have psychological practice licensing laws restricting use of
the term to those persons who have earned a Ph.D. in
psychology, had several years of carefully supervised clinical training, and passed a licensing examination designed
to test clinical competence (some states grant the very
same license, however, to psychologists in other applied
areas, such as industrial, social, educational, and counseling psychology).

Psychologists can be particularly helpful in assessing
clients and in suggesting ways to help the people you
counsel. Since psychological evaluation, including psychodiagnostic testing, is pretty much the exclusive province of
the psychologist, you may want to have a clinical psychol-

ogist assess your more difficult or puzzling clients. Or you may want to have him routinely see all of your counselees. Through this kind of preliminary screening, he can recommend specific helping procedures for each person and can also determine which clients need medical (i.e., psychiatric) attention. A psychologist who does a significant amount of consulting will usually be happy to meet regularly with you for informal review and discussion.

Social workers and rehabilitation counselors: Although most social workers and rehabilitation counselors work for agencies rather than privately, they can still be of much help to you. They will frequently answer questions by phone and can refer you to additional sources of help when appropriate. Social workers are usually able to provide information on public service resources and can answer questions about such matters as state and county aid and the availability of free medical and psychological care. Rehabilitation counselors are customarily well versed in vocational matters, such as job training program requirements, and they are able to help with career decisions and adjustments. These few sentences do not list all the services these specialists provide, but I have mentioned the ways they may be of most assistance to you as a clergyman.

How to pick a good consultant: I would like to offer a few tips on how to choose a professional consultant. First, select someone with whom you feel comfortable working. If you live near a large city, there will be many consultants from which to pick, so be discerning. You may want to try several consultants until you find one or two you prefer. Second, be direct and clear in telling a potential consultant exactly what you want. If you don't, there are bound to be misunderstandings and resentments. Third, give your consultant reactions to what he does for you so that he has every opportunity to be maximally helpful. Fourth, in choosing and collaborating with someone, don't use your clients as go-betweens to obtain information about yourself. If you want to ask a personal question, go ahead and do so, but don't edge around the issue. Most professionals are willing to talk openly with you about whatever personal concerns you may have, but they resent manipulation and indirectness. So, to sum up these suggestions, trust your instincts in choosing consultants and be honest in dealing with them.

Psychological Testing

In the past, clinicians relied heavily on psychological tests and so almost everyone who received psychological services was tested. Over the past two decades, this practice has declined so that now, as a rule, only certain individuals are given psychodiagnostic testing. The change has occurred partly because of expense, partly because of doubts about the usefulness of blanket testing, and partly through a change in the professional *Zeitgeist.*

I recommend this: (1) refer for comprehensive testing only those persons with whom you will be working for an extended time; and (2) refer for more limited testing those persons who are particularly puzzling to you or those who you suspect have a more serious disorder than is immediately apparent. Since psychological testing can be expensive, you ought to have a clear idea of what you want to know, i.e., make sure the referral question is unambiguously stated. This will help you obtain the information you need and will guard against unnecessary expenditures by your client. Normally only psychologists are competent to administer and interpret psychological tests, particularly those which assess aspects of personality. I have briefly summarized below the more commonly used tests.

Wechsler Adult Intelligence Scale (WAIS): This is an individually administered I. Q. scale that contains eleven subtests, both verbal (e.g., general information, comprehension of everyday situations, vocabulary, and mental arithmetic) and nonverbal (e.g., puzzles, indicating missing parts to incomplete pictures, and cartoon sequence arrangement). The WAIS gives a verbal, a nonverbal ("performance"), and a composite intelligence quotient.

Wechsler Intelligence Scale for Children (WISC): The WISC is the children's counterpart to the WAIS, covering the age range from five to sixteen. There is also a Wechsler scale for preschool and primary age children (the WPPSI).

Stanford-Binet Intelligence Scale: This is the grandfather of individually administered I. Q. tests and is still widely used with children (although it can also be administered to adolescents and adults). The Stanford-Binet contains many subtests, arranged in order of ascending difficulty, and it takes about the same time to administer as the WAIS, WISC, or WPPSI (an hour and a half).

Wide Range Achievement Test (WRAT): Requiring only about twenty minutes to administer, the WRAT yields measures of basic academic achievement in the form of grade level scores for reading (word recognition), spelling, and arithmetic.

Bender Gestalt Test: This quickly administered test consists of nine line drawings which the person is asked to copy. It is most commonly used to assess perceptual-motor functioning and sometimes indicates the presence of brain damage.

Rorschach Inkblots: Of all psychological tests, the Rorschach has been both the most publicized and the most controversial. It takes about an hour to administer and consists of ten complex inkblots which the person views one at a time. He tells the psychologist what each one looks like to him and, later, the parts and qualities of each blot to which he attended. Since the test cards merely show inkblots, whatever the subject "sees" is thought to reveal his personality. Critics of the test claim that its utility depends more on the interpretive skills of the psychologist than on the test results themselves.

Thematic Apperception Test (TAT): For this test, the subject makes up stories to a set of standard pictures. The psychologist evaluates these stories, usually with reference to the themes they depict (e.g., nurturance, aggression, dominance, and sexuality) and to how conflicts are managed. Like the Rorschach, the validity of the TAT has come under attack, but in my opinion a seasoned clinician can obtain useful information with these techniques.

Minnesota Multiphasic Personality Inventory (MMPI):

The MMPI is a paper-and-pencil test consisting of over 500 items, each of which is answered either true or false by the subject. It can be administered in groups and machine scored, and yields results that can be integrated into a personality profile.

Personal Interview: Face-to-face interview material is almost always an important part of psychological assessment. Psychological tests, contrary to popular belief, do not give infallible results and they are not "psychic x-rays." I will not dwell here on the content of an assessment interview, as we have covered this material earlier in the chapter.

Basic Interviewing Techniques

Principles of psychological interviewing could easily fill an entire volume (e.g., the book by Bugental recommended at the end of Chapter Two). Nevertheless, I would like to discuss briefly some of the more basic principles of conducting counseling interviews. Every counselor has to find the methods that work best for him, but these guidelines may help you find the professional style with which you are most comfortable.

There are very few fixed rules for doing good interpersonal work and there are even fewer universally applicable techniques. To do your job well, you must tailor your approach to fit the individual client. So be flexible and trust yourself. No person or book can surpass the sensitive and concerned judgment of a counselor who is actually sitting across from a client. In reading this section remember that *you* are in the best position to make decisions about your work. Adopt my recommendations only to the extent that they feel right to you.

From Questions to Statements

The earmark of a naive counselor is that he asks too many questions. He feels compelled to keep things moving and, in trying to accomplish this, cuts off any real immersion in the counseling process. It is difficult to get out of the habit of overzealous questioning, so you may have to make a conscious effort to do so. Try tape recording a few of your interviews (with your client's permission, of course). Notice how you handle silences. Do you immediately rush in with a question to avoid the discomfort of a long pause? Listen to how you respond to expressions of feeling. Do you ask a question that focuses attention on some surrounding circumstance and thereby draw your client away from his affect? Or do you respond in a manner that facilitates personal expression? In general, try to move from asking questions, which tend to be intrinsically demanding, to making statements, which usually allow a client much more autonomy and security. Remember that your job is to facilitate, not to interrogate.

Nonverbal Messages
Another mistake some counselors make is ignoring nonverbal communication. They attend too much to *what* the person says and thereby miss *how* he says it. This emphasis on content to the neglect of style is severely limiting to a counselor. How a person says what he does, as well as how and when he grimaces, fidgets, blushes, stammers, and stiffens, are vitally important cues which qualify, sometimes tremendously, the meaning of his words. These, and not his sentences, are the key to your client's feelings. So be observant. Learn to watch and hear the message behind the words. Harry Stack Sullivan used to recommend to his students that whenever anyone said anything to them in psychotherapy, they ask themselves what else the person could possibly mean. Extreme? Perhaps. But there's a good lesson in it nonetheless.

Directness versus Brutality
It is fashionable these days to "say it like it is," and, for the most part, I value this trend as a needed corrective for a culture which has institutionalized deceit. Most of what we call tact and diplomacy is either euphemized dishonesty or coldblooded manipulation. Nevertheless, I am troubled that the new openness has been vulgarized. Directness has, for some, become an excuse for brutality. And in counseling, brutality is fatal. So say what you see, but do it caringly and with a sense of good timing.

The Value of Self-Disclosure

Self-disclosure means giving someone privileged access to your private life or to your secret thoughts, feelings, and attitudes. For example, most men would not readily tell you their yearly incomes; most women would hesitate discussing their sexual history; and very few people of either gender would easily reveal their psychological problems or family slander.

Self-disclosure by a counselor can have a number of benefits, as long as it is appropriate and succinct. Revealing yourself to your client can: (1) help build the counseling relationship by demonstrating your trust in the client; (2) provide a model of interpersonal openness; (3) show the client that his problem is not unique and that his feelings are "OK"; and (4) facilitate *his* self-disclosure through what has been called the dyadic effect, i.e., people tend to reciprocate self-disclosure if it is not too intense or unexpected. So opening up to your counselee can be beneficial in a number of ways. But long personal stories tend to draw him away from himself, turning his awareness toward you or, what's worse, toward abstract and emotionless chatter. Make sure your disclosures are relevant and to the point and that they are not intrusive.

Dealing with Resistance and Blocking

The best way to respond to mild blocking is with patience. Just be casual and tolerant. If the blocking takes on the quality of resistance — like the client digging in his heels and opposing you — you might try telling him that you sense he is retrenching and, in the process, asking him if he has a similar impression. If he doesn't, don't fight it. Sit and wait, behaving as easy and unassuming as you honestly can. If, on the other hand, your client is aware of resisting you, all the better. Encourage him to get the feel of what he is doing. Maybe even tell him to resist you actively so that he can move to a position of accepting responsibility for his resistance and bringing it under voluntary control. If the person is overtly hostile to you or adamantly resistant, don't try to break through his barriers unless you're fairly sure you know what you're about.

Reflections and Interpretations

I want to preface this section by pointing out that counselors are frequently much too concerned with reasons and too little concerned with actualities. Looking for psychological causes can be helpful if it is more than editorializing and intellectualization. But usually it is not. Most efforts to figure out why someone feels the way he does only serve to help him avoid feeling it. Keep in mind that most people you will be working with are disconnected from their feelings and that your task is to facilitate a reemergence and revitalization of the parts of themselves they are avoiding.

Reflections are saying back to the client the essence of what he just expressed to you. Sometimes you need merely to repeat his own words and other times you have to paraphrase, boil down, and rework what he has told you, in light of his expressions, prior comments, and so on. For example, a person might say, "Nothing has much meaning for me. I'm tired and I've never found anything to really hold my interest. Life hardly seems worth it." Among the many reflective responses you might make would be "You haven't been able to take hold, to get much enjoyment out of life." Such reflections can facilitate further self-exploration and immersion in counseling.

While reflections are efforts to recapitulate and, as such, remain fairly close to what the counselee has actually expressed, interpretations are more speculative. They are explanations to the client of why he feels, thinks, or acts as he does, usually with reference to his childhood. An interpretation would be, "You are afraid of women because your mother was distant and unloving, and you never had the chance to experience female warmth." While this might be true, saying it may not help the person experience himself better or get over his fearfulness. So interpret sparingly, if at all, or you'll wind up in fruitless discussions about the origins of problems without ever doing much about them.

The Use of Homework

Recommending something for your client to do or to think about between sessions is often helpful. This serves to give him a more active part in his own growth, decreases dependence on the counseling session, and helps him integrate what he does during the counseling interview with the events of his daily life. I sometimes suggest specific behaviors for the client to try, making it clear that it is his decision whether or not actually to do them. Other times I merely suggest that he observe some aspect of himself during the day. The list of possible homework suggestions is virtually endless, so you may want to try giving various kinds of homework.

Reassurance and When Not to Offer it

As noted in Chapter Two, reassurance is not always helpful to a client. It can be ineffective and even alarming, particularly to suspicious persons, who are often made more fearful by it. Except at points of genuine crisis, elaborate reassurance is best avoided. Be warm, but don't be too reassuring because this can have the effect of denying or blocking out the seriousness of a client's concerns. A person to whom you say, "Everything will be all right" might well say back, "But you don't hear me." A related problem involves premature affirmations. For example, the assertion, "You've got a good marriage" makes it difficult for some clients to mention their marital difficulties.

Staying with the Counselee

Counseling is a process and, like any other process, can be relatively smooth and efficient or stormy and inefficient. The counselor has only limited control over the course of counseling, but to the extent that he resonates with his client, he will foster an effective working relationship. The best way to facilitate a client's personal exploration is to treat him with quiet, aware reverence. Suspend all other concerns and attend to him with your whole being, very much like a Zen master. Listen. Hear. Feel. Sense. Intuit. Touch without touching. To do this requires that you can exist in the present, without jumping to the future or the past. By so doing you will curtail one of the major enemies of good counseling, your own anxiety. You must be prepared to give up your "therapeutic serenity," however, if the need arises. Some people require that you take affirmative action on their behalf — for example, an individual who is acutely psychotic. Becoming an effective counselor involves learning when and when not to take direct supportive action.

Record Keeping and Note Taking

It is a good idea to keep brief records of when you meet with a person as well as of significant developments during counseling. This will allow you to review your work periodically and thereby to get a better grasp of how your client is progressing. It will also provide you with a self-training program in that you can study the effectiveness of your interventions.

The question sometimes comes up as to whether or not a counselor ought to take notes *during* a session. This is useful the first session or two when you are gathering background information, but after that I recommend against it. You cannot fully attend to the present if you are busy writing down the past. And it tends to annoy some clients and to make others suspicious. There are a few occasions where it is helpful to make a note or two while you are counseling. For example, if you suddenly recall something you have to do, it is better to jot it down than to ruminate over it for the remainder of the session. But on the whole, I suggest that you do your writing after the session.

Preview

In this chapter I have tried to present as much practical information about counseling as possible, including discussions of client evaluation, relationship structuring, and interviewing principles. Chapter Four will deal with special clinical techniques, such as behavior modification and group counseling, and with common though difficult problems, such as suicide threats and alcoholism.

Recommended References

Benjamin, A. *The Helping Interview*. Boston: Houghton Mifflin Company, 1969.

This short and easy-to-read book elaborates many of the themes presented in the latter part of this chapter, and it makes an excellent companion volume to Bugental's *Psychological Interviewing* (see Chapter Two). Benjamin gives advice on such matters as structuring a helping relationship, facilitating a client's self-exploration, and dealing with defensiveness and other obstacles to counseling.

(Paperback; about $3)

Cronbach, L. J. *Essentials of Psychological Testing*, 3rd ed. New York: Harper and Row, 1970.

If you are interested in taking up the topic of psychological tests in more detail, this textbook is probably a good place to start. Cronbach, who is one of the deans of American psychology, discusses the various kinds of tests, their respective assets and liabilities, and criteria for evaluating the merits of any proposed psychological measure.

(Hardcover; about $11)

Steinzor, B. *The Healing Partnership: The Patient as Colleague in Psychotherapy*. New York: Harper and Row, 1967.

Steinzor offers an enlightening view of the helping process from the vantage point of a psychotherapist. He writes about the practical problems one encounters in doing psychological work and considers such questions as the extent to which therapists actually help their clients and the doubtful validity of several beliefs and practices which have been traditional in this field.   (Hardcover; about $6)

CHAPTER IV

SPECIAL TECHNIQUES AND PROBLEMS

Special Techniques
Knotty Problems

IN THIS FINAL CHAPTER I would like to discuss a number of clinical techniques which may prove useful to you in your counseling. These include crisis intervention procedures, behavior modification, emotional facilitation methods, and group counseling. We will also briefly consider two medical treatments with which you ought to be familiar, psychiatric hospitalization and the use of psychoactive medications such as tranquilizers and antidepressants. Finally, I would like to offer some practical suggestions on how to respond to a number of particularly challenging behavior problems, such as alcohol abuse, suicide threats or attempts, assaultive behavior, and sexual difficulties.

Special Techniques

Before beginning our coverage of special counseling techniques, I want to emphasize that I am not advocating the indiscriminate application of methods that properly fall within the province of the trained psychotherapist. Yet I believe that many times a clergyman can appropriately and effectively use clinical methods, provided they are intelligently woven into the fabric of on-going counseling relationships. As we go along, I will provide guidelines to help you decide when and with whom to use a given technique. Although these will include relevant cautions, keep in mind while using any of these methods that a conservative decision-making policy is best, i.e., when in doubt, don't use the technique.

Crisis Intervention

One way of viewing a crisis is that it is an experience of unusual psychological distress which threatens the person with inadequacy. During a crisis, the individual's normal means of handling stress prove insufficient and he is forced to develop new ways of coping. Regarded in this manner, a crisis is not necessarily harmful and, in fact, may become the vehicle of significant personal growth. For example, consider a young woman whose recently drafted husband has been sent overseas. Even though his departure may upset her considerably, it may also prompt her toward greater strength and self-sufficiency. In this case, the "crisis" may turn out to have been one of the most constructive events in the woman's life. There is a well-developed literature concerning crisis intervention, and as someone on the beachhead of a great deal of crisis work, you might want to look into it. The most I can do here is to suggest ways of squeezing a crisis for maximum psychological mileage — of putting the person's pain to good use for him.

Most experts feel that a crisis period usually lasts from four to six weeks and that, during this time, the individual is maximally open to change. Because of this, the counselor can be most effective if he works with the client before he passes out of his agony and back into his previous modes of adjustment. To illustrate the kinds of life events that can precipitate a crisis, consider: loss of a loved one; damage to or loss of a bodily part; financial ruin; legal difficulties; occupational failure; damage or loss through natural disasters such as fires or earthquakes; serious health problems such as major surgery or chronic illness; romantic disappointment; and, for young children, school changes or sibling births.

In assisting a person in crisis, it is usually best first to help him understand exactly *what* is troubling him and *how* it developed. Along with this, try to provide a climate that allows the client to vent his feelings, whether grief, rage, fear, or whatever. At the same time, do not pressure him to emote since he may view his reactions as irrational if not bizarre. A person in crisis is ordinarily frayed emotionally and he is likely to become frightened by strong feelings. It is therefore best to be accepting but not demanding in your crisis work.

Some crisis specialists recommend a problem-solving approach and regard the crisis predicament as a challenge to be met and a puzzle to be figured out. This is a cognitive rather than an affective orientation, and an important part of this approach is mobilizing available family and community resources so that the person obtains whatever environmental support he needs. Most large cities have several crisis intervention centers, and it is a good idea to have their phone numbers and addresses handy. This will enable you to refer promptly persons with whom you do not feel comfortable working, and will also give you quick access to professional advice — an especially valuable asset when dealing with self-destructive people.

Behavior Modification (Behavior Therapy)

The fields of clinical psychology and psychiatry have undergone something of a minor revolution over the past twenty years. Whereas traditional psychotherapy and counseling have been oriented around the client's subjective experience, "behaviorists" try to alter behavior without attending much to unobservable mental events (see "Counseling as Habit Change" in Chapter Two). This kind of approach to clinical problems is becoming more and more popular, partly as a result of increasing dissatisfaction with treatments that take years to produce desired results.

The term "behavior therapy" (which incidentally is a more narrowly defined term than "behavior modification," even though I am using them interchangeably) has been applied to a number of very different techniques, some of which are not nearly as free of mentalism as their advocates suggest. Nevertheless, they all focus on the "symptom" itself rather than searching for deep-rooted intrapsychic causes. In fact, to a behaviorist the word "symptom" is a misnomer because it implies the existence of an underlying disease which doesn't exist — the symptom is the disease! Whether or not you agree with this view, you can make good use of the empirical fact that behavioral methods work well for at least certain kinds of problems. The nature of these problems will become clearer as we proceed.

Contingency management: People often behave maladaptively because they get a payoff for doing so, i.e., they are subject to a contingency which specifies that they will be rewarded (or, alternatively, will not be punished) if they perform the maladaptive act. To make the discussion more concrete, consider: (1) Johnny, who is ten years old, gets a stomach ache whenever he is lonely because his parents attend to him most when he is sick; (2) Mrs. Jones breaks her furniture because her husband then takes her more seriously; (3) Sally, age 15, frequently threatens to leave home because this frightens her parents into meeting her demands; (4) Mr. Smith remains quiet at work because his co-workers criticize everything he says; and (5) Mr. Doe drinks heavily because then his otherwise uncaring wife worries about him. Notice the word "because" in each example, reflecting that they all involve a contingency, an "if-then" relationship.

One of the most fruitful things you can do in counseling is to discover which consequences maintain which behaviors. You can then set about altering the harmful contingencies or, at very least, bringing them to light. To return to our last example, you might restore harmony in the Doe household plus save Mr. Doe's liver by getting his wife to pay more attention to him when he's sober and to ignore him when he's drunk. I recommend the book edited by Krumboltz and Thoresen entitled *Behavioral Counseling: Cases and Techniques* (see references) for detailed advice on contingency management and related behavioral methods.

Desensitization: This is a technique for reducing avoidance behavior by alleviating the fear or anxiety that maintains it. Desensitization is based on the rather simple principle that tension and relaxation (or some other "competing response") are incompatible and that if you can teach the person to relax in response to the feared object or activity he will no longer react to it with anxiety — in fact, he cannot since anxiety and relaxation are mutually exclusive.*

---

*There has been some challenge to the assumption that relaxation and anxiety are incompatible, but the issue is too complicated and esoteric to warrant discussion here.

There are a number of ways to do desensitization, but for the moment we will focus on a simplified version of Joseph Wolpe's "systematic desensitization" (references to Wolpe's work appear in Krumboltz and Thoresen). First have the client sit in a comfortable chair with his eyes closed and his hands in his lap, and then relax him by saying something like this in a slow, soft voice:

Become aware of yourself as you sit in the chair. Feel your arms and legs, the weight of your body, and your shoulders and your lips. Get the feel of your eyes, your face, your head, your ears, your mouth, your neck, your chest, your stomach, your abdomen, your lower body, your legs, and your toes. Become aware of whatever tension exists in your body and see if you can allow it to dissipate. Feel your neck and shoulders and allow them to relax. Become aware of whatever tension exists in your face and let it go. Now see if you can feel yourself lying in a warm bath . . . hot, tired, lazy. Feel yourself warm and listless. Now see if you can feel yourself floating on a cloud . . . light, weightless, and free.

You will have to practice doing this in your own words and at your own pace. If you have willing friends, practice your relaxation method on them.

Once the client is relaxed, ask him to imagine the very mildest confrontation possible with the feared object or situation. For example, if your client is afraid of speaking before an audience, ask him to imagine addressing a very small audience for just a few moments. Then, proceeding slowly enough not to disrupt his relaxation, have him imagine speaking to a slightly larger audience for a slightly longer time. By gradually progressing up such a graded list of confrontations, you can often ameliorate simple fears in short order.

There are a number of cautions to be observed, however. You ought to refer to a psychologist anyone who has a serious phobia (see Chapter One), particularly if the feared object is suggestive of mental disorder (e.g., blood, knives, burglars, rapists, etc.). Although these sorts of phobias may be relatively insignificant for specific individuals, in others they may be highly symbolic and pathological.

Secondly, a person who either is seriously disturbed or has strong concerns about maintaining control should not be desensitized without the presence of a trained clinician.

Live fear-reduction techniques: A useful alternative to the method we have just considered is desensitization using the concrete object or situation. For example, if someone is afraid of elevators or of dentists you might reduce or even alleviate his fear by going with him as he gradually approaches an elevator or the dentist's chair. The effective principle here is the same as in armchair desensitization, i.e., replacing anxiety responses with relaxation or confidence, which in this case has been fostered through your support and reassurance. Bear in mind, as before, to proceed slowly and let the client set his own pace.

Normally I think it is better to use *in vivo* (live) over imaginal desensitization whenever possible because it is less mental and more tied to concrete reality. Furthermore, the *in vivo* method embodies an additional therapeutic ingredient, modeling. That is, you as the counselor are setting an example of nonfearful behavior for your client to imitate.

Mental rehearsal: Another variation on systematic desensitization is mental rehearsal without relaxation training. Although the reasons are not yet understood, merely rehearsing in one's mind the performing of feared activities seems to lessen the intensity of the fear associated with these activities. There is evidence that this treatment, developed by Milton Wolpin of the University of Southern California, works as well as systematic desensitization.

Just have the person close his eyes and imagine himself doing what he fears. Try to get him to visualize it as realistically as he can and encourage him to feel himself into the imagined scene. Even though you ought to proceed slowly, there is no need to run through a formal hierarchy of graded tasks, nor to concentrate on lengthy relaxation training. As with systematic and *in vivo* desensitization, I have used this guided imagining technique with good success. I would recommend, however, that you use one of the first two treatments unless you·are sure your client is quite stable. This is because, in my opinion, the client's psychological experience is a little harder to predict or control with pure mental rehearsal than with a form of desensitization that firmly structures mental events, either through a series of graded scenes or through actual interaction with the feared object.

Role playing and assertive training: Still another related technique is role playing — having the client practice the desired behavior with you in the office. This method can be adapted to a number of problems and it is particularly suited to teaching a person how to speak up for himself. The best way to do such "assertive training" is to alternate roles with your client. One time let him be the asserter and then switch. Try to work up to the point where both of you are acting assertive simultaneously, thus giving him practice "under fire." Have him pretend, for example, that you are a resistant waiter who has just brought him an undercooked steak. After he is facile at insisting that you return it for further cooking, let him practice sending back an overcooked steak (which requires more assertiveness since this demand necessitates preparation of an entirely new meal). The main caution to observe, once again, is to proceed slowly, bearing in mind that if one member of a family suddenly becomes assertive, the other members are likely to react strongly — the same is true of the client's employer!

Emotional Integration Methods
(Gestalt Therapy)

Gestalt therapy is a highly specialized art which requires years of training to perfect. Nonetheless, you can profitably use some of the ideas and techniques that have grown out of Gestalt. For detailed exposition, see the book by Perls, Hefferline and Goodman cited at the end of the chapter. Here I will highlight those aspects of Gestalt which are likely to be most valuable to you in your day-to-day counseling.

Being one's tears or whatever: Most people in our culture grow up to regard strong feelings as annoying disruptions to be eliminated or, better still, avoided. Many of us have thereby learned to dwarf our humanness by splitting off vital parts of ourselves — our sadness, our joy, our grief, our anger, our ecstasy, or our love. One of the finest ideas to come out of Gestalt therapy is the value of re-uniting a person with these alienated aspects of himself.

For example, many people come for counseling all choked up, trying to fight back tears which they see as a sign of weakness or pathology. For the most part, however, it is not tears but the suppression of one's tears that is pathological. Will Rogers said it well, "We think too much and feel too little." Most of us try to cognize our way out of our feelings, and so the person on the brink of tears is more likely to analyze *why* he feels tearful than simply to cry. And so it goes for almost any strong emotion. Unfortunately, many therapists continue to foster this self-defeating intellectualization by encouraging the person to editorialize about the reasons for his emotions rather than helping him connect with them.

The upshot of all this is that it is desirable to facilitate your client's expression of himself, especially his emotions, and to avoid lengthy and superficial analytical discussions. Point out to him how he inhibits his expression, for example by stiffening his face or breathing tightly, and communicate that it is helpful to vent his feelings. The best way to communicate this is to express your own feelings unobtrusively. If you are moved by what you see in your client, go ahead and let your eyes get misty. Just do it in a quiet way that doesn't turn the spotlight of the counseling relationship on you.

In terms of cautions, never force your client to emote, because this may frighten him away or, worse yet, precipitate a serious psychological upset. Also, do not use an affect-oriented counseling approach with a very disturbed or even marginally adjusted person since such a person does not need any further loosening up of his already faltering inner controls. His emotions have already broken out, albeit in an unwholesome way.

Making mental conversations explicit: As I pointed out

in Chapter One, people say all sorts of unreasonable things to themselves, most of which they have learned from "significant others" such as parents. Furthermore, most of us are only vaguely aware of our inner conversations. You can sometimes help a person merely by having him act out the parts to his dialog. For example, have him sit in a chair and verbalize one voice of a dialog, perhaps "You really loused up that relationship. You should have kept your mouth shut like I told you." Then have him move to another chair facing the first and respond, perhaps "Get off my back. I said what I said and that's all there is to it. Don't tell me what I should have done." Have him then return to the first chair and continue the dialog (which in this case reflects an internal power struggle). Most clients have difficulty doing this and experience what Perls called "'stage fright." Others find it alarming and strange. So ease into it, giving the client time to adjust to the procedure.

Group Methods

Group techniques are becoming increasingly popular, both with professionals and laymen. This is partly because more people can be treated per unit time in groups than individually and partly because the social pressures and reinforcements that operate within groups can be put to good therapeutic use. Although you may or may not find use for group methods, depending on the size of your counseling load, I will briefly discuss a few of the more important principles of group work so that you will have them available. Then we will consider group therapy and the new group forms, variously called growth, sensitivity, laboratory, training (T-), and encounter groups.

Group counseling: The main thing to remember in doing group work is that the whole is different from the sum of its parts. In other words, a group has a life of its own, a unique chemistry which may not be what you would have expected from knowing the individual participants. The second point to keep in mind is that your job is not to direct group interaction but gently to guide and clarify it. Allow the group to direct itself and to develop its own

processes. Intervene only if it is getting too rough or re-
maining too superficial. Finally, do not put anyone who is
seriously disturbed into a group, because not only does
this represent a potential source of disruption to the group
but it also entails a risk to the person himself. Someone
who shows significant psychiatric disturbance is likely to
find a group experience both alarming and damaging unless it is conducted by a seasoned clinician who knows the
in's and out's of conducting groups for seriously disordered
people. In fact, the best way to learn how to do any kind
of group counseling is by working with a competent group
leader. Many psychologists and psychiatrists would be glad
to have you sit in on some of their groups.

Group therapy: There are many different styles and approaches to group therapy in current use. Some therapists
focus on group process — they point out the subtleties of
interpersonal dynamics and expose manipulation and indirectness as it occurs. Other therapists do what amounts to
individual therapy in groups, so that the bulk of interaction
in such groups is between the therapist and one other
member. Some therapists focus on outside problems which
participants bring up in the group, while other therapists
disallow such discussions and attend only to what happens
between group members. Some groups are scheduled for a
set number of sessions, and others are open-ended. I think
you can see that different professionals run very different
kinds of groups.

The new group forms: While group therapy is presumably oriented toward the remediation of problems, the new
group forms (encounter groups, sensitivity training, etc.)
are not. Rather they are designed to foster personal growth
in people without noteworthy psychological difficulties.* A
whole subculture has grown up around such groups on the
West Coast, and the "touchy-feely" lifestyle has become
almost a religion. This fadism, together with the offbeat
extensions of this lifestyle which frequently pervade the

---

*I regard this distinction as by-and-large a specious one. In my opinion,
some of the new group methods, if employed by a competent leader, are
more therapeutic than much of what continues to be called group therapy.

mass media, have turned off many persons who might otherwise have profited greatly from participation in a well-run group. The problem comes in when Arthur Amateur, who has had the sole benefits of a freshman psychology course and some personal pathology, decides to conduct a group for persons worse off than himself. Unfortunately, in most states there is very little control over this sort of thing and the would-be group leader can usually avoid legal trouble by being careful not to use words like psychology, psychiatry, or psychotherapy. So check out the credentials of the proposed group facilitator and remember that even a well-credentialed professional may not be adept at running groups. In groups where the leader is sensitive and knowledgeable, a great deal of good can be accomplished.

Psychiatric Medications

The advent of psychoactive drugs has revolutionized psychiatric care. Less than thirty years ago, a person showing serious psychiatric disturbance was almost certainly destined for confinement and repressive treatment. Today, however, many such persons are able to lead relatively normal lives on maintenance doses of psychiatric medications. Since there is assessment (diagnostic) value to knowing something about the medicines a person takes, I will survey some of the more commonly prescribed psychiatric drugs.

Tranquilizers and sedatives: There are two main types of tranquilizers, major and minor, and they are distinct both chemically and in terms of their effects. Most of the major tranquilizers belong to a class of chemicals called phenothiazines and they are usually prescribed for persons who show signs of serious psychiatric disturbance. They have the very desirable effect of calming down the disturbed person without putting him to sleep. Among the more frequently administered phenothiazines are Thorazine (chlorpromazine), Stellazine (trifluoperazine), and Mellaril (thioridazine). The minor tranquilizers are usually given to less distressed persons to reduce anxiety and physical tension. Among those commonly prescribed are Librium (chlordiazepoxide), Valium (diazepam), and Miltown or Equanil (meprobamate). To illustrate how this information can be helpful in your evaluation of a client, imagine that you are interviewing a person who shows only mild distress but who tells you he is taking Stellazine. This should alert you to the possibility of a more serious problem than is immediately apparent.

Sedatives are sleep-facilitating medications and are of both barbiturate and nonbarbiturate types. The clinical effects of sedatives and minor tranquilizers are similar (in fact, some physicians feel the latter ought to be classed as sedatives). Examples of barbiturates are phenobarbital, pentobarbital, amobarbital, and secobarbital. (See the section on "Chemical Dependencies" in Chapter One for a discussion of some of the dangers associated with the use of barbiturates.)

Antidepressants: These are of several chemical types and are prescribed for depressions ranging all the way from mild to severe. They are sometimes quite effective in alleviating depression, but unlike the other drugs we have considered, antidepressants often take from a few days to two weeks to produce the desired results. Frequently used antidepressants are Aventyl (nortriptyline), Elavil (amitriptyline), Marplan (isocarboxazid), Norpramine (desipramine), and Tofranil (imipramine).

Sometimes antidepressants and major tranquilizers are administered conjointly. For example, Etrafon and Triavil both contain amitriptyline, an antidepressant, and perphenazine, a phenothiazine. These drugs are given when the person shows a mixture of depression and other psychiatric symptoms.

A new group of drugs containing small amounts of the metal Lithium are gaining widespread acceptance as effective antidepressants, particularly for persons who undergo wide mood swings. Many physicians view the new Lithium compounds as very promising, especially for the long-term maintenance of individuals who experience recurring bouts of depression.

Stimulants: These drugs are employed for a wide range of purposes, from the relief of mild depression to use in the emergency room of a hospital. Perhaps the most frequently prescribed stimulants are the amphetamines. Like other stimulants, they accelerate bodily processes and are still widely administered as diet pills (although many physicians deplore this practice). Examples of amphetamines are benzedrine and dexedrine. A non-amphetaminic stimulant called Ritalin (methylphenidate) is also in common use, and it often produces a paradoxical (calming) effect on children.

Psychiatric Hospitals, Suicide Prevention Centers, and Other Community Resources

Despite the decline in the frequency of psychiatric hospitalization recently brought about by psychoactive drugs and new community mental health centers, it continues to be necessary to provide hospital care for many individuals. If a person is a danger to himself, through faulty judgment or suicidal intent, or if he is dangerous to others because of irrational behavior or homicidal inclination, he ordinarily requires confinement. Even people who do not represent a danger to themselves or others are sometimes hospitalized voluntarily because, in the opinion of the attending psychiatrist, they can be best treated through brief hospitalization. Good psychiatric hospitals offer a much more elaborate program of therapy than can usually be provided in an out-patient setting, and are temporary shelter from the pressures of daily living.

It is a good idea to know the location of a nearby public psychiatric hospital so that you can take people for examination and possible medication and/or hospitalization when it becomes necessary. Most county hospitals have psychiatric evaluation units and these are an excellent back-up resource for a counselor.

It is also wise to know the phone number and location of the nearest suicide prevention center. Most large cities have such facilities and they can be exceedingly valuable as an emergency resource. Mental health clinics are also worth locating so that you have a place to refer individuals in need of low-cost therapy. Finally, free clinics can be useful, especially for persons with drug problems.

Knotty Problems

Depression and Suicide

Over 30,000 people commit suicide every year in this country and at least ten times that number attempt it. Many of these attempts are undoubtedly pleas for help or "gestures," and some successful suicide attempts were never meant to succeed. Yet, a substantial number of our citizens show serious self-destructive intent and need competent and efficient professional attention. A far greater number, although not suicidal, are significantly depressed and need psychotherapy.

Origins and signs of depression: There are several psychodynamic mechanisms which can underlie depression, but before outlining them I want to mention a distinction frequently made by psychiatrists, between exogenous and endogenous depression. The former is precipitated by a specific life event and is hence a reactive, psychologically determined depression. Endogenous depression, on the other hand, is not caused by an identifiable event, is much more cyclic in nature, and is considered more biological in origin. Although this distinction may ultimately prove arbitrary, it does suggest that depression is a complicated symptom which may have significant physical underpinnings.

One of the most common psychodynamic explanations of depression is that it is inverted anger. Instead of directing his anger toward the person(s) who caused it, the individual turns it on himself. Another view of depression is that it is the product of withdrawal and its accompanying restriction of involvement, all of which retards both psychological and biological processes. Still another theory is that depression results from an unresolvable conflict, such that the person will suffer painful consequences regardless of what he does. Seen this way, depression represents a kind of psychological freezing in the face of severe conflict. Finally, I believe that some depressions occur when a person feels intense sadness, grief, or sorrow and does not express it. Depression in these instances reflects a holding back, a constriction of oneself. More important than understanding the causes of depression is being able to recognize it when you see it. In addition to self-reports of feeling depressed, self-demeaning statements, and psychomotor retardation (slowed speech, movements, and thought processes), clinicians look for three biological signs of depression: reduced appetite and recent weight loss; diminished sexual interest; and sleeping difficulties. Keep in mind that while the presence of these signs usually indicates the existence of significant depression, their absence does *not* imply its non-existence. The same is true of the psychological signs given above. In fact, some people manifest a "smiling depression" in that the more depressed they become, the happier they look.

Assessing suicidal risk: The best overall rule here is to refer the person to a clinician whenever you have reason to suspect suicidal intent or ideation. There are a number of high suicide risk indicators and I will review some of them here for you. A divorced person is a higher risk than a widowed or single person, who in turn are higher risks than a married person. Women make more attempts than men, but men have a much higher suicide rate (three times that of women). People who live alone are high risks, as are those in the involutional years (women above age 45 and men above age 55). However, adolescent and young adult suicides are on the rise. A rejecting or instigating family member — one who challenges the person to "go ahead and do it" — suggests a high risk as does recent loss of a loved one, job, or good health. A definite plan is suggestive of high risk, and finally, the intended use of a gun, rope, explosives, or jumping is more suggestive of risk than is a plan involving gas or pills.

What to do with an acutely suicidal person: If you believe that a particular person is acutely suicidal, it is imperative that you face the problem head-on and leave nothing to chance. In the event that someone calls you and says that he is about to commit suicide or that he has just overdosed, the first thing to do is to find out exactly where he is. You can then summon help and ensure that it gets to the person without delay. If your community has a fire and rescue squad, you might call them and pass on the information. They will normally be able to respond to the emergency effectively and efficiently. Other alternatives are that you call an ambulance or the police, depending on the nature of the intended action.

When someone comes to your office and expresses the same intent, you are in a better position to assess him and to decide, on the basis of your assessment, how to proceed. If the person is willing, you might just as well take him either to a private psychiatrist or to the psychiatric unit of a county hospital for evaluation. Many times the person will be treated as an outpatient; but if he is judged to be an immediate danger to himself, he will be temporarily hospitalized. If he has already taken an overdose of drugs, you may need to call an ambulance. In cases where the person resists such measures, you have no alternative but to call the police, who will ordinarily escort the individual to a hospital. Although this may prove embarrassing to the person, the alternative may be far worse.

Sexual Problems

There are a host of sexual deviations, such as fetishism (sexual gratification through contact with an object such as stockings or underwear), transvestism (gratification through dressing in clothing of the opposite sex), and pedophilia (child molesting). These are all complicated problems which warrant referral to a psychotherapist, as does homosexuality.* We are concerned here with a different set of

---

*I am assuming that the individual regards his deviation as a problem requiring remediation. The American Psychiatric Association recently voted to delete homosexuality from its official list of mental disorders. For those persons who are distressed by their sexual orientation, the APA now applies the term "sexual orientation disorder." One of the imports of this decision is to keep morality and psychiatry separate in the matter.

problems — the kinds of sexual difficulties that can crop up in the life of just about any normal person.

Impotence: The inability to achieve and/or maintain an erection is a fairly common male sexual difficulty and it occurs for a variety of reasons. Fatigue or emotional stress is a frequent cause. A less obvious cause is resentment toward the man's wife, especially if she is emasculating. Often he will be impotent only in relation to her but not toward other women. Full sexual response requires the ability to soften emotionally, and it is difficult to do this in the midst of a cold war. Clinicians talk of two types of impotence, primary and secondary, according to whether or not the man has ever been able to get an erection. If you know that the husband has been able previously and you are fairly certain that his problem is psychological, direct counseling toward remedying it if possible. For example, try to get him to express his hostility toward his wife in some other way. Just remember that most men are very touchy about their sexual adequacy, so tread carefully.

Premature ejaculation: Ejaculating before his wife can achieve climax is another common male sex problem. At first glance, this might seem to be the opposite of impotence, but the two are actually closely related. As with impotence, fatigue or emotional constriction can play a causative role, as can resentment since premature ejaculation is an excellent way to frustrate (punish) one's wife. Behavioral conditioning can be important too. Consider a man whose wife's vagina is easily irritated and who frequently exhorts him to "get it over with." It is easy to see how he might develop a maladaptive response pattern. Finally, the condition of premature ejaculation is a relative one in that it is defined in relation to another person's responsiveness. Obviously if the woman has trouble reaching orgasm, the man's ejaculatory response will almost always be premature.

If you believe the problem to be of emotional origin, try to determine the basis of it. Focus your efforts on altering this underlying condition. However, if you do not get fairly rapid improvement, refer the couple to a reputable sex clinic, an option you can exercise in the case of any sex problem that does not show signs of improvement. Part of the initial work-up at these clinics is a physical examination. *Frigidity:* The female counterpart of impotence is frigidity, the diminution or absence of sexual response. Total frigidity is rare and refers to the complete absence of arousal. Partial frigidity, which is much more common, refers to an inability to reach climax or extremely slow excitability. Like impotence and premature ejaculation, frigidity is frequently of emotional origin and such factors as exhaustion or anger can diminish a woman's responsiveness. Another factor seems to be fear of men and of sexuality. To the extent that frigidity in a particular instance is temporary, you might be able to ameliorate it with emotionally oriented counseling.

Vaginal tightening: Reflexive constriction of the vaginal barrel because of anxiety is also common, particularly during the first few months of marriage. If the problem does not show signs of diminishing, the couple should consult a sex clinic or a behavior therapist who has had experience treating the condition. Encouraging the husband to be patient is also helpful.

Counseling Juveniles

Working with juveniles is a challenging specialty. Minors develop problems unique to their age groups, and they are normally less able than adults to verbalize psychological experiences. Consequently, approaches to counseling children often differ from those used with adults. As the age of a particular child increases, he will ordinarily show a corresponding gain in verbal expressiveness; but once the child reaches puberty, this gain is offset by the renewed turmoil of adolescence. Even experienced psychotherapists often refer children to a child specialist, so you may find yourself doing the same with many of the youngsters who are brought to you. In this section I would like to discuss the problem of assessing child and family problems, along with some of the considerations you ought to observe in counseling juveniles.

Assessment: When parents ask you to help their child, you need to assess the nature of the problem and how it relates to the family as a unit. Often you will find that your evaluation of the problem does not correspond to the parents' assessment, and in general the difficulty they describe will fit into one of several categories. I will go over these in some detail.

First, the parents may believe that their child has a problem simply because they are unfamiliar with the behavior of other children his age. For example, parents of a nine-year-old may be distressed because he wants to spend countless hours away from home with his best friend. Upon inspection, the child may turn out to be quite normal. The parents may need merely to be advised that children his age frequently form a close relationship with a special "chum" and that not only is this to be expected, but it is desirable since such friendships serve as correctives for idiosyncratic thought processes. Counseling in such instances consists of teaching the parents what to expect of their child and of reassuring them of his well-being. Appropriate reading materials or observations of other children can help considerably.

A related but more complex problem arises when the parents are unreasonable in their demands and expectations, even after they have become familiar with the normative behavior of the child's age-mates. Usually such parents are more rigid than most, which compounds the difficulty because they will also prove to be more defensive. I think you will be amazed, if you are not already, by the extent to which certain parents regard their offspring as extensions of themselves and by how persistently they intrude into their lives. Nonetheless, parents who regard their child as little more than a satellite are not likely to benefit from your telling them that, at least not right away. The best way to help is to build a strong enough relationship with the parents so that, in time, they can begin to open themselves to the possibility that the child may be a person in his own right and that he can be trusted with some self-direction. You can normally accomplish this by "giving slack" in your counseling, i.e., by hearing out their concerns and acknowledging their legitimate expertise in the matter as the parents of their child. Then gradually — perhaps over the course of several months — you can begin to "wonder if maybe" they are being "just a tiny bit" too demanding. If they seem open to this possibility, you can reiterate it gently during the next few sessions, until they begin to catch on and explore the issue for themselves. Hopefully you will find that they start to connect with their own insecurity and how they direct it *at* the child — rather than coming to grips with their anxieties and impulses, they project them onto the child and then control *him!*

A still more difficult situation emerges in families where one member serves as a scapegoat for the rest. For one reason or another, this particular person — often a child — is chosen to be "it" in a pathological game of tag. Whether or not he manifests psychiatric disturbance, the family perceives him as responsible for everyone's troubles. And in some highly disturbed families, whatever psychopathology the child does manifest has been actively cultivated by the others in order to maintain him in his appointed position. Usually this serves some immediate function in the home, such as diverting the family's attention away from serious marital problems, and it may give one or more family members a target at which to throw the blame for personal failure. These kinds of family dynamics are difficult to change, and if possible it is best to refer such families to psychotherapists. In cases where the family is unwilling to follow through on such a referral, see them regularly and slowly ease into the business of reflecting back to them what you see. But proceed cautiously and give them only as much reflection as they can comfortably tolerate, since you will probably lose the family if you move too quickly . . . and this would be unfortunate indeed for the poor child who is the designated scapegoat.

Another type of family pattern you will encounter is one in which the child is genuinely misbehaving but his parents are at wits' end over what to do about it. The difficulty is often compounded for well-read, psychologically minded parents who have absorbed all sorts of conflicting advice — "never punish," "dare to discipline," "foster self-expression," "set firm limits," "offer the child choices," etc. If the child's problem seems to be simple misbehavior, such as leaving his toys all over the house or refusing to come in when he's called, you might want to use behavior modification methods (see "Contingency Management," p. 104). I have found it helpful to keep on hand copies of Gerald Patterson's *Living with Children* (revised edition by Gerald R. Patterson and M. Elizabeth Gullion. Champaign, Ill.: Research Press, 1971), which sells for about three dollars. This is a programmed manual for teaching parents how to change their child's behavior effectively and humanely, and it has greatly assisted many a frustrated parent. If for one reason or another you believe that the parents would not study the book and follow through with its recommendations, you might want to go over it with them chapter by chapter. In families where the youngster is an adolescent, you might also want to use the sequel to *Living with Children,* entitled *Families* (by Gerald Patterson, also Research Press, 1971). The latter manual contains procedures appropriate for use with older children but it presupposes some knowledge contained in the other book.

Still another family situation confronts you when the child shows obvious personal disturbance, such as severe anxiety, withdrawal, depression, or aggressiveness, or such behavior as fire setting, unusual cruelty, repetitive stealing, continual running away, bedwetting (enuresis) beyond age five or six, severe nail biting, or delinquency. In these instances, you ought to try to get the parents to consult a child psychologist or psychiatrist. Sometimes parents are afraid to do this because they expect to be blamed for the child's difficulties — they expect the doctor to ask them something like what the young lad with F's on his report card asked his dad, "Is it heredity or environment, Pop?" In actual fact, most therapists are very supportive, especially during the first session, and they are not at all interested in fixing blame. Nevertheless, you may want to

accompany the family on their initial visit in order to provide them with the support of your presence. Many times
what at first glance appears to be a serious problem will
turn out to be a minor one; but for the child's sake, the
family should give him the benefit of at least one consultation.
Specific syndromes of childhood and adolescence: I
would now like to discuss some of the specific disturbances
that frequently show up in the lives of juveniles. It would
take volumes to treat adequately child and adolescent
psychology, but I can at least provide you with an overview of some of the more common youth disorders.

Thousands if not millions of children have been labeled
hyperactive (hyperkinetic) because they show exaggerated
restlessness, irritability, distractibility, and general unruli-
ness, particularly in structured settings like the classroom.
As such, the term "hyperkinesis" is merely descriptive of
such behavior. But often the word is taken to imply that
the child suffers from "minimal brain dysfunction," and
many times there is no basis for this belief other than his
agitated behavior. It is easy to see the circular reasoning
here: "Why does the child act up? Because he has brain
dysfunction. How do we know that? Because he acts up."
The danger in unreflectively calling children hyperactive is
that then they are regarded as organically impaired — sick
— rather than as children who need to be taught more
appropriate and adaptive behaviors. Application of the
term "hyperactive" is many times just one more instance of
the nominal fallacy, i.e., generating the illusion that you
understand something through the mere use of a technical
word. My point is that many of the "hyperactive" children
you encounter will probably not be suffering from organic
dysfunction but rather from the effects of adverse experience. Their behavior reflects emotional disturbance and/or
bad training, not central nervous system impairment. On
the other hand, it must be recognized that there are children who do suffer from such impairment and whose behavioral difficulties clearly mirror this. These children
require medical evaluation and follow-up, and they frequently have to take daily medications to calm them down.

Ritalin (mentioned earlier under "Stimulants") is often prescribed. Although it stimulates adults, it exerts the so-called paradoxical effect on children of quieting them. In practice, regardless of whether or not an agitated child is physically impaired, he can benefit from learning better concentration skills and more internal control. The operant conditioning techniques described by Patterson and Gullion in *Living with Children* are well suited to accomplish these goals.

While hyperkinesis is primarily a childhood disorder, adolescents are the group who most often show the kind of aggressive, antisocial behavior we call delinquency. There is a somewhat arbitrary but nonetheless crucial distinction between the youth who gets in trouble primarily because of group influences and the one who needs no such encouragement and who is well on his way to developing a counter-social personality (see Chapter One). The former is capable of personal loyalty and involvement, and even strongly felt responsibility — in fact, it is exactly such loyalties, involvements, and responsibilities that foster his delinquency because they are centered around the wrong people. The latter is calloused, insensitive, superficial, and hurtful. He is usually unable to profit from experience and repeatedly runs afoul of social sanctions. Obviously, it is generally easier to effect positive change in the life of the first (dyssocial) youth than in that of the second (countersocial) one. Often the dyssocial youngster is getting his psychological needs met outside the family and is in essence fleeing a nonrewarding home life. Dramatic effects can sometimes be obtained by working with the family to restructure their interactions so that the deviant youth finds more emotional fulfillment within the home. In cases where the adolescent has a long history of aggressiveness, unpredictability, and impulsiveness, no such abrupt turnarounds are to be expected. But you may still be able to help by encouraging the parents to communicate clear and consistent rules and expectations to the youth. This can teach him better self-control and more appropriate behavior, and may in time foster better conscience development and interpersonal sensitivity, especially if the parents can be taught to exert their controls in a loving manner. What has sometimes happened in the lives of delinquents is that their parents have not learned effective ways to manage them, which in turn has led to a great deal of resentment toward the child. The build-up of such resentment, with its usual accompaniment of hostility and withholding of affection, produces an emotional hardness in the youngster. A complication that more and more often enters the clinical picture is drug use. Refer to the relevant sections of this chapter and Chapter One for discussion of this problem.

Several other disturbances occur frequently enough with juveniles to warrant mention. Some children withdraw into themselves and become overly quiet and difficult to contact emotionally. Sometimes this happens because the child has been traumatized in some way or other, but it also occurs in children who have never learned how to share themselves because everyone in their immediate family is distant and unexpressive. You may be able to help such a youngster greatly by spending time with him and gradually teaching him to express his thoughts and feelings. This learning can be facilitated by your sharing your own thoughts and feelings, provided that you do not overwhelm him. It may be helpful to refer back to the section on the seclusive personality in Chapter One for further guidelines on counseling withdrawn youths.

Occasionally you will run across a child who seems anxiety laden if not terrified most of the time. This problem must be assessed carefully, and I recommend that you routinely refer such children to a psychologist or psychiatrist for evaluation. If this is not possible, plan on spending many hours of "comfort time" with the youngster and, along with this, see if you can determine what, if anything, is going on in the family to perpetuate his suffering. In cases where you can isolate specific fears and where you feel comfortable doing so, you might want to build some desensitization into your counseling (see p. 104).

Finally I want to comment briefly on youths who repeatedly run away. Usually they are high-strung, impulsive persons who cannot tolerate interpersonal conflict or who have learned to intimidate their parents with threats of fleeing. Frequently they are loners who also show other kinds of misbehavior such as stealing or sexual promiscuity. These juveniles ought to be referred to a psychotherapist, unless you are fairly certain that the runaway episodes are simply manipulative and that you can curtail such blackmail by family counseling. In instances where the youth is primarily uncomfortable with interpersonal closeness (rather than manipulative) and where he cannot see a therapist for one reason or another, you might be able to help by forming what amounts to a surrogate parent relationship with him. In this relationship you can begin to teach him to face conflicts and to tolerate anxiety sufficiently so that he no longer has to take flight during stormy times at home.

When to see whom: Whenever you decide to provide services yourself, either because the presenting problem does not warrant formal psychotherapeutic attention or because the family has refused to accept referral, you must decide whether to see the youth alone, the parent(s) alone, both the child and parents together, or some combination of these. And at times, you may elect to work with the entire family, including siblings.

I recommend that, for the initial interview, you see the parents and the child together, with or without siblings depending on their ages and the nature of the problem. This will allow you to observe interactions within the family and to categorize the difficulty in terms of the scheme I presented earlier under "Assessment." Beyond the first session, whom you see ought to be determined by whether you conceive of the problem as primarily individual or familial. Naturally most juvenile disorders have their roots in the dynamics of the family, but many youth problems have become functionally autonomous (Gordon Allport's term) in the sense that they now exist within the personality of the child and are no longer maintained by domestic events. The decision you make regarding whom you will see has some fairly obvious symbolic consequences, i.e., ordinarily you will be perceived as an ally of the child, an agent of the parents, or a consultant and arbitrator to all. Allow me to survey quickly some of the different circumstances that might lead you to make one decision or another.

If you feel that the child's problem is amenable to remediation by the parents, provided they implement the necessary changes, you might choose to see them alone to supply the requisite advice and encouragement. For example, the father may be heavily invested in his work, to the neglect of his family. The mother in turn may resent this, and the child may be reacting to both his neglect and her irritability by getting into minor troubles outside the home. His difficulties may clear up if the parents are counseled and if they are willing to change the pattern of their marriage, e.g., the husband agrees to spend more time and energy at home and the wife agrees to find ways of increasing his incentive to do so, perhaps by learning how better to satisfy his emotional needs. Another example of when it might be appropriate to work only with the parents would be if the child is simply misbehaving and they need training in how to deal with this.

Alternatively, you may find that the youngster needs a confidant and validator. This is often the case with young adolescents, who are normally groping to find a stable identity, which by the way is largely the reason they are so clothes-conscious and form cliques. The routine turmoil of adolescence can develop into distressing personal concerns and can result in significant family upset, so you may do much good by providing the youth with genuine understanding and well-placed advice. However, if you choose to fulfill this role you ought to observe a couple of cautions. Do not talk about the boy or girl to his parents unless he or she is present. Adolescents are particularly sensitive to anything that can be interpreted as betrayal or as an adult coalition against them. Also, along the same lines, avoid going along with efforts by the parents to engage you in "clinical conferences." These usually begin with, "There's a little something I wanted to ask (or tell) you about Jamie." So that you do not alienate the parents by limited responses to their questions, you ought to tell them in advance how you would like to handle the problem of private conversations and why. Lastly, do not minimize or take lightly the feelings of an adolescent (or a child for that matter). They are just as vulnerable and easily hurt as we are, in fact more so, and they are often acutely sensitive to patronizing attitudes.

Finally, you may come to the conclusion that the family is the appropriate object of counseling. I have already discussed some of the guidelines to observe in working with particular types of family problems, and I have just one to add here. If you choose to see the family routinely as a unit, it is normally best to see them together and to avoid talking with any member without the others present, at least about matters of counseling. Otherwise you may find yourself being played off by one or more parties against the others. There are a few instances in which you might effectively work with the youth and the parents separately, but I suggest you do this only after carefully weighing the relative advantages and disadvantages.

Assaultive Persons

Usually there are only two kinds of people who are likely to prove assaultive, either someone in a paranoid state or a countersocial person with a history of poor impulse control who has a motive for hurting you (e.g., robbery or rage). Although it is difficult to offer definitive advice on how to handle combative persons, I would like to comment briefly on the matter and suggest some ways for you to behave in the clinch.

In dealing with a threatening person, you have to make some rapid assessments and decisions. You must first evaluate the earnestness of the threat — does the individual intend to carry it out — and then you must consider the lethality of the threat — is he intending, for example, to smack or to shoot you? In any event, it is not appropriate for you to take careless chances that are likely to lead to injury. Neither should you act in such a manner that the person is likely to be hurt if this can be avoided. The optimal resolution, of course, is that the potential assailant desists and that he verbalizes the feelings he was previously intending to act out.

In most instances, it is best to respond to threats matter-of-factly. Maintain a low profile in the transaction and expect the unexpected. Answer questions directly, if and when they are asked, but do not pressure your potential opponent by asking *him* questions or by otherwise stimulating him with unnecessary words. If the individual is grossly delusional, for example if he thinks that you are Satan or if he accuses you of plotting against him, take the threat seriously because you are very likely in real danger. If the person presses you for replies to his accusations, tell him factually that you are not who he thinks you are or that you have not done what he believes. But leave it at that and in no way argue with him. Delusions tend to become even more fixed when they are challenged, so stick to simple, nonargumentative statements. Do not try to win the individual's confidence either, because suspicious persons are usually very frightened by warmth and intimacy. Finally, it is my belief that you should never attempt to physically subdue a potentially dangerous person unless your life or someone else's is in imminent danger.

Alcoholism

Alcoholism has been conceptualized in several different ways, but I think the most useful definition is this: alcoholism is the condition in which the consumption of ethanol (ethyl alcohol) regularly impairs the person's mental, behavioral, or physical functioning. About ten million Americans have serious drinking problems, so that alcoholism is a major national health concern. Well over ten percent of first admissions to psychiatric hospitals are due to alcohol abuse.

Before proceeding, I want to emphasize that alcohol, when used in large quantities over prolonged periods, damages both the central nervous system and vital organs such as the liver — and it fosters addiction. The implication of this is that a person with a drinking problem is, roughly speaking, suffering from a disease and that the choice of whether or not, and particularly how much, to imbibe is largely beyond his control. Consequently, as most counselors discover, exhortations to "straighten up and stop your drinking" are generally futile. Some authorities believe that such encouragements only aggravate the problem by playing into the "alcoholic dynamic," i.e., not only does it reinforce (via attention and concern) the deviant behavior, but it also validates the alcoholic's life role of loser and martyr. Effective treatment of problem drinking must deal either with the consumption behavior directly — which is virtually impossible except in a controlled environment — or with the underlying psychological disturbance. As a counselor, you are limited to the latter approach. This is a difficult job requiring skill and patience, especially since alcoholics are usually spasmodic in treatment.

Patterns of problem drinking differ widely, as do the routes by which individuals become alcoholics. Some people, for example, drink daily for years, are nearly always mildly intoxicated, and yet never act outlandishly. As a result, they are rarely identified as problem drinkers and continue to poison themselves unnoticed. Housewives and female divorcees often manifest this pattern of ingestion, and although men still show a much higher incidence of alcohol abuse, alcoholism in women is definitely on the rise. Other people go on "benders" during which they become thoroughly inebriated. Often these persons initially limit their drunkenness to "lost weekends" but are later unable to prevent such episodes from infringing on the work week. An alarming amount of job absenteeism in this country is directly attributable to alcohol intoxication. Still other people combine these two patterns in some fashion, for example by drinking in the course of their employment (client entertainment, etc.) and then finding that they no longer stop at two or three drinks but sometimes continue until they are robustly ossified.

Some people become dependent on alcohol through gradually increasing their intake. They begin as light social drinkers and progress to heavy, compulsive ones. Others develop an alcohol problem as a reaction to a painful crisis, such as loss of a loved one, financial ruin, or occupational failure. Still others have significant psychological problems to begin with and learn to drink heavily as a way of reducing psychic discomfort (anxiety, depression, and the like). In any event, regardless of the particular course through which excessive drinking develops, most alcoholics share a number of personal qualities. Although there is probably no such thing as a specific "alcoholic personality," the majority of problem drinkers are emotionally dependent, self-oriented, immature, and somewhat passive. They also have a distinctly limited ability to tolerate psychological anguish, which makes them especially prone toward reliance on anxiety-reducing substances — unfortunately, ethanol is one of the most effective anxiety-reducers sold over the counter. Furthermore, despite the social flair demonstrated by some alcoholics, as a group they are unable to maintain intimate relationships. Putting all this together, it is clear why alcoholism has been described as a symptom that has become a disease.

There are a number of alcoholic syndromes, ranging from simple drunkenness to delirium tremens (DT's), alcoholic paranoia, various vitamin deficiency disorders frequently associated with chronic alcohol abuse, and abnormally strong reactions to small quantities of alcohol. Delirium tremens occurs in persons who have been chronic heavy drinkers, usually for many years, and it is characterized by delirium, including hallucinations (usually visual, olfactory, and tactile), and by tremors which may or may not be localized to a particular part of the body. The disorder is thought to occur as a withdrawal syndrome, i.e., as a reaction to a decrease in alcohol intake after prolonged use, and it is sometimes characterized by the interesting behavior of the alcoholic picking imaginary bugs off his body (called formication). Some alcoholics show a similar delirium syndrome without the termulousness of DT's. Alcoholic paranoia is a state of severe suspiciousness, occurring most commonly in males. They frequently suspect their wives of unfaithfulness and sometimes act on their suspicions by harming the spouse or her presumed lover. Many psychiatrists feel that the alcohol merely serves to unleash an already existing paranoid disturbance. Certain nutritional deficiencies, particularly of the B vitamins, can cause serious and irreversible brain damage when these deficiencies continue over a long period of time. Although the diseases (e.g., Korsakov's — or Korsakoff's — psychosis and Wernicke's syndrome) are not caused by ethanol *per se,* alcoholics frequently suffer from the vitamin losses that do induce them. Alcoholic deterioration, also primarily caused by vitamin deficiency, sometimes occurs in persons who have used alcohol heavily for many years. It is characterized by gradually progressing brain destruction resulting in personality deterioration. Finally, some persons respond to relatively minute quantities of alcohol with an abrupt, psychotic-like reaction. Expert opinion favors the view that, as in the case of alcoholic paranoia, the chemical serves only to set off a preexisting disturbance, in this case a seizure-like disorder (disorganized firing of brain cells, usually called a convulsion).

You can appreciate from this survey of syndromes that alcoholism is by and large a medical problem and that it is by no means a simple disease. Few problems are both as frequently encountered and as difficult to treat successfully.

Counseling an alcoholic is a tricky matter because it requires that you offer enough support to help him stay dry but not enough so that you become embroiled in what I referred to above as the alcoholic dynamic. Not only does this dynamic involve your validating the alcoholic's pathological self-concept, but it usually also includes an endless alternation of sobriety and drunkenness, with the spouse (or clergyman!) continually "rescuing" the drinker (see Berne's discussion of this in *Games People Play,* referenced at the end of Chapter Two). In the long run, such rescuing with its customary sequel of lecturing only serves to worsen the condition.

In working with a problem drinker, first determine if *he* views his drinking as a problem. If he does, try to help him find alternate ways of dealing with emotional discomfort, such as talking with someone (but not a drinking buddy!) or scheduling a counseling appointment. Along with this, see if you can build up his tolerance for confronting un-pleasantness. In other words, teach him that he can face his upsets and that he does not need to retreat into alcoholic oblivion. Do this by encouraging him to express his frustrations, embarrassments, self-doubts, angers, griefs, conflicts, or whatever. Facilitate emotional expression, as opposed to mere talk, wherever possible, and be sympathetic. Just avoid becoming a savior yourself or you will probably be ineffective. If you suspect that the person is suffering from a physical disorder of any sort, such as one of those mentioned above, make sure that a physician (psychiatrist, internist, or general practitioner) examines him.

In cases where the person does not regard his drinking as a problem — and this is common — you have to make a difficult choice: either accept his point of view temporarily and deal with other matters in counseling, or try to get him to accept yours. The best way to do the latter is to "build your case" over a period of time, and then present it. For example, make note of the times when he is clearly intoxicated and gently use this information to confront him about his ailment. When skillfully done, this kind of "case presentation" can turn a person's life around by getting him to accept his problem, years before he might do so on his own. Unless an individual acknowledges his alcohol dependence, you are unlikely to alter it. However, some people need time and personal assurance to come to grips with their problem, so don't rush it. Organizations such as Alcoholics Anonymous (AA) are frequently helpful because they provide an accepting atmosphere in which the person can truly face himself.

Physicians have been using certain drugs, for example Antabuse (Disulfiram, or tetraethylthiuram disulfide), to treat some alcoholics. These chemicals interfere with the normal metabolism of alcohol, resulting in an accumulation of one or more intermediate breakdown products, which in turn make the person violently ill. This treatment is superb in concept — it's simple, inexpensive, and relatively safe. Unfortunately, it frequently fails to work in practice, primarily because it requires that the patient cooperate in taking the medication daily. Since the drug does nothing about the underlying psychological condition that precipitates the heavy drinking, such cooperation is rarely forthcoming. Counseling and/or psychotherapy remain the primary treatments of choice.

Drug Problems

In Chapter One, we considered some of the chemicals that are commonly involved in drug problems, from narcotics to amphetamines, barbiturates, and psychedelics. It may be helpful for you to reread quickly the section in that chapter dealing with chemical dependencies. I would now like to discuss some further aspects of drug abuse and then offer a few guidelines on how to respond to acute drug problems.

Many of the comments contained in the last section concerning alcoholism are applicable to drug dependencies. There is an important difference between alcoholism and many forms of drug abuse, however, namely that while alcohol ingestion is socially sanctioned to the extent that liquor can be purchased in almost any grocery store, the use of drugs is not. With adolescents, because of the many youth drug subcultures that develop, the significance of this distinction is perhaps diminished. Nonetheless, you will probably find that the drug users you encounter are somewhat more countersocial than are alcoholics, although the latter group certainly contains its fair share of angry, abusive persons.

Chemical dependencies can arise in a number of different ways, and various drugs tend to enter the lives of people in characteristic fashions. Heroin, for example, is never medically prescribed and therefore can only be obtained on the illegal market. Consequently, most heroin addicts become users through close association with one or more other users. Another opium derivative, morphine, is sometimes prescribed to alleviate severe pain, and many people have become addicted to it as a result of its availability during an illness. Alternatively, it can be obtained on the streets. As with heroin, tolerance develops such that the individual requires increasing amounts of the substance to produce the same effect. This quirk in biochemistry escalates the monetary price of maintaining a heroin or morphine habit, and it drives many people into lifestyles of crime (robbery, prostitution, etc.). Demerol, a synthetic analgesic (pain reliever) commonly used as a presurgical medication, is also addicting, and it and other drugs like it are often used illegally by hospital personnel. Cocaine, like heroin, is a street drug.

As discussed in Chapter One, barbiturates are commonly prescribed as sleep-inducing medicinals. Like narcotics, they produce tolerance effects, and as a result, persons who are abruptly taken off large doses of barbiturates sometimes show withdrawal symptoms such as delirium and convulsions. Nonbarbiturate sedatives such as Doriden (glutethimide), Placidyl (ethchlorvynol), and Quallude (methaqualone) seem to be gradually supplanting the older barbiturates in medical practice, but unfortunately they also show addicting properties. Closely related to these drugs are the so-called minor tranquilizers such as Librium (chlordiazepoxide), Valium (diazepam), and Miltown or Equanil (both trade names for meprobamate). The minor tranquilizers too are widely prescribed and frequently lead to dependence in persons who use them routinely. An older class of drugs called bromides used to cause many addictions, and you may still run across a case of bromide dependence today. But this is unlikely since the barbiturate and nonbarbiturate sedatives and tranquilizers have largely supplanted the prescription of bromides.

Marihuana (grass, pot) is now in common though illegal use, but it is not addicting. Nevertheless, many youths become so dependent on it that they can scarcely go through a day without using some. Its main effects are euphoria and a distorted time sense. True hallucinogens, such as LSD (lysergic acid diethylamide), psilocybin, and mescaline are also illegal and are not addicting in a formal sense (i.e., no tolerance development and no withdrawal symptoms upon abrupt termination). Yet they are dangerous because they can produce severely frightening experiences which the user relives over and over again, even months later (these are usually called streaks or flashbacks).

Amphetamines, as outlined in Chapter One, continue to be prescribed as diet aids. They are not addicting, although many people become dependent on them as stimulants (they are called "uppers" while barbiturates are called "downers"). Amphetamines can produce bizarre if not psychotic-like behavior in certain persons and consequently they are not as harmless as many people think. Yet these drugs are readily available on the street market.

Sniffing (glue, gasoline, lighter fluid, cleaning liquids, and the like) has become a popular, though dangerous pastime among youths, particularly withdrawn delinquents. Though these substances are not formally addicting, they can produce serious damage to the central nervous system and the body.

Having reviewed the substances that are most often involved in chemical dependence problems, I would like briefly to discuss treatment. Ordinarily there is very little you can do as a counselor to cure someone of a true addiction or a heavy dependence. Consequently, drug problems involving the regular use of any of the following substances will be difficult to remedy in counseling: narcotics; barbiturates; nonbarbiturate sedatives and tranquilizers; prescription analgesics; bromides. If the person is using the substance only irregularly, you may be able to ward off an impending addiction or dependence, but once he has become genuinely "hooked," the problem is physical (i.e., medical) rather than psychological.

Persons who are indulging in the regular use of amphetamines, marihuana, or hallucinogens, or who have been inhaling toxic chemicals, may be helped considerably by regular counseling. Bear in mind that the use of chemicals is customarily a symptom of underlying psychological disturbance, such as strong conflict, low self-esteem, high anxiety, depression, or rage. Drug users frequently show very little capacity to tolerate anxiety, so that you must be prudent in your efforts to activate latent feelings. Well-modulated emotional support is an important aspect of effective counseling with people who rely on chemicals. I would now like to offer some guidelines on how to respond to persons who manifest acute drug intoxication:

(1) If someone is obviously delirious, see that he gets immediate medical evaluation, preferably by a psychiatrist in a hospital setting. I recommend that you take the person to the hospital yourself if he is willing and if you feel comfortable doing so. If you have reason to believe that the person has overdosed on a harmful substance, get him to a hospital however you can, regardless of his preference in the matter (i.e., call an ambulance if this is indicated).

(2) If the person has taken psychedelics and is having a "bad trip," provide reassurance and stay with the individual. However, if the drug has precipitated a full-blown psychotic episode, see that he gets to a hospital, preferably the psychiatric evaluation unit of a nearby county facility if one is available.

(3) If the person is clearly a danger to himself or others and will not consent to going to a hospital, call the fire and rescue squad in your community, if one exists, or summon the police. Although involving law enforcement officials is best avoided in counseling, someone who represents a danger leaves you no alternative if he will not consent to hospitalization.

In many communities, voluntary drug help centers will provide emergency assistance at any time; you should have their phone number on hand. Often they can send persons familiar with drugs to "talk down" someone experiencing a bad reaction to drugs, and without introducing the fear of prosecution.

Recommended References

Golembiewski, R. T., and A. Blumberg (Editors). *Sensitivity Training and the Laboratory Approach: Readings About Concepts and Applications.* Itasca, Ill.: F. E. Peacock Publishers, 1970.

This is an excellent survey of the ideas and techniques of some of the new group forms we considered in this chapter. It is rich in source material and many of its contributors are well-known group experts.

(Hardcover; about $10)

Krumboltz, J. D., and C. E. Thoresen (Editors). *Behavioral Counseling: Cases and Techniques.* New York: Holt, Rinehart and Winston, 1969.

This book is full of practical tips on how to use behavioral methods in your counseling. Contributed articles cover such problems as underachievement, procrastination, social anxiety, and excessive fears. I strongly recommend that you look through this book if you can. (Hardcover; about $10)

Parad, H. J. (Editor). *Crisis Intervention: Selected Readings.* New York: Family Service Association of America, 1965.

Both theoretical and case material on crisis work are presented in this volume. It well represents the kinds of orientations adopted by crisis experts.

(Paperback; current price unavailable)

Perls, F., R. F. Hefferline, and P. Goodman. *Gestalt Therapy: Excitement and Growth in the Human Personality.* New York: The Julian Press, Inc., 1951.

If I had to recommend a single book for a counselor's personal growth and professional maturation, this would be it. Although the book deals with therapy rather than counseling, it contains a tremendous amount of information which is valuable to counselors. It also includes personal growth experiments (exercises) for the reader.

(Hardcover, about $8; also available in paperback for about $3)

Index